DISCOVERING REPTILES

by Kelly Gauthier

Illustrated by Julius Csotonyi

APPLESAUCE PRESS

KENNEBUNKPORT, MAINE

13-Digit ISBN: 978-1-64643-051-2
10-Digit ISBN: 1-64643-051-4

This book may be ordered by mail from the publisher.
Please include $5.99 for postage and handling. Please support your local bookseller first!

Books published by Cider Mill Press Book Publishers are available at special discounts for bulk purchases in the United States by corporations, institutions, and other organizations. For more information, please contact the publisher.

Applesauce Press is an imprint of Cider Mill Press Book Publishers
"Where good books are ready for press"
PO Box 454
12 Spring Street
Kennebunkport, Maine 04046
Visit us online!
cidermillpress.com

Typography: Antique Olive, Block Berthold, Destroy, Gipsiero, Imperfect, PMN Caecilia

All vectors used under official license from Shutterstock.com

Printed in China
1 2 3 4 5 6 7 8 9 0
First Edition

TABLE OF CONTENTS

INTRODUCTION

Snakes that slither, chameleons that change color, lizards that laze in the sun—and so much more! There are thousands of species of reptiles in the world. Really, *thousands*. Scientists (the ones who study reptiles are called herpetologists) have named more than 11,000 different species in more than 90 different families of reptiles. That's a lot of reptiles, but some common names you might recognize are snakes, lizards, turtles, and crocodiles. Reptiles have been around for a lot longer than humans. Reptilian ancestors can be traced back 315 million years. That means a lot of dinosaurs were reptiles! And the dinosaur ancestors of modern reptiles also have another modern species that came

from them—birds. Modern birds share tons of common traits with reptiles, but they're warm-blooded instead of cold-blooded.

So what makes reptiles different from other animals? To start, reptiles are air-breathing animals (yes, even the ones that spend time in the water). And reptiles are all vertebrates. That means that they have a spine just like you do, even snakes. Their skin is something that makes them unique, and it's the biggest difference between reptiles and amphibians like frogs. Reptiles have a thick layer of skin that's covered in scales (or larger bony plates called scutes), which makes them kind of look like they're wearing armor. Their skin is almost like a wetsuit. It helps to keep water out, which lets reptiles spend time on land and in the water. But that skin isn't permanent. Reptiles actually shed their skin; a new layer of skin forms underneath the old skin, and fluid builds up beneath the old skin and pushes it off. With snakes, this process can be really dramatic. The skin comes off from head to tail, so it looks like a whole new snake is emerging. With other reptiles it's not as noticeable since the shedding happens in patches.

The biggest difference between reptiles and mammals, like humans, is that reptiles are cold-blooded. Unlike warm-blooded animals, reptiles can't maintain their internal temperature in different environments. If they want to warm up, they move into the sun; if they want to cool down, they move into the shade. But in the winter when the weather is cold they can't stay warm like people can, so many reptiles become inactive when it's too cold. That's right, they hibernate.

Most reptiles lay eggs, excluding some types of snakes that give birth to live young. Those eggs are laid in nests, and although there are a few reptiles that stay near the nest until the eggs hatch, most just leave the eggs where they are without watching them. Unlike bird eggs that need to be protected and kept warm by their parents, reptile eggs can survive just fine on their own in the nest. The temperature of the nest around the eggs actually determines whether the reptiles in the eggs will be male or female. And once they hatch, the reptiles are small but fully formed and ready to go out into the wild on their own.

Get ready to learn about the wide world of reptiles, from the biggest to the smallest, from the most well-hidden to the brightest, and from the most common to the rarest. You might be surprised by what you discover.

CHAPTER 1

SEA TO SKY: REPTILES EVERYWHERE

You might not notice the reptiles all around you, but they live everywhere, all over the world. Reptiles can be found on every continent except Antarctica, and they can survive in just about every environment. They live burrowed deep underground or up in the tops of trees. They can be found in swamps and deserts and rainforests.

Everywhere you look, there are reptiles big and small making their home in nature. And even though they're not naturally aquatic or airborne, there are reptiles that have adapted to swim in the sea and glide through the air.

PIG-NOSED TURTLE
CARETTOCHELYS INSCULPTA

LOCATION: Australia and New Guinea

AVERAGE SIZE: 20 to 25 inches (50 to 63 centimeters)

REPTILE REPORT: Oink, oink. The pig-nosed turtle is named because of its long, fleshy snout with pig-like nostrils. This freshwater turtle lives in the rivers, ponds, and creeks of Australia and New Guinea. What's even more interesting than this turtle's nose is its front limbs. They're paddle-like flippers, which is something that's much more common in sea turtles than freshwater turtles. Those flippers are useful in the water, but they're not great for walking on land, so the pig-nosed turtle spends much more time in the water than out of it.

This species of turtle has an impressive family tree that extends back 140 million years. That means its ancestors were around at the same time as dinosaurs! They're omnivores, and they'll eat mollusks and insects along with fruit, leaves, and flowers.

LEATHERBACK SEA TURTLE
DERMOCHELYS CORIACEA

LOCATION: Atlantic Ocean, Pacific Ocean, Indian Ocean, and the Mediterranean Sea

AVERAGE SIZE: 5 to 6 feet (1½ meters)

REPTILE REPORT: How long can you hold your breath? The leatherback sea turtle can hold its breath underwater for up to 85 minutes—remember, they breathe air, so that's a really long time! They can dive much deeper than any other turtle (and deeper than most other ocean animals), going as far down as 4,000 feet (1,220 meters). These are the largest turtles, as tall as an average human (if not taller) and weighing in at more than 1,000 pounds (453 kilograms). Leatherbacks don't have a hard shell. Instead, they are flexible and leathery, giving them their common name. Most turtles are too cold in the deep waters where leatherbacks feed. Unlike other turtles, which can't keep their bodies much warmer than the water around them, leatherbacks keep themselves warmer than the water thanks to a layer of fat and a unique blood vessel structure that helps them retain heat better than other reptiles.

Leatherback turtles migrate between breeding and feeding areas, and their travels can take them around 4,000 miles each way. To the north, they'll go up to Canada and Norway, and to the south they adventure to New Zealand and South America. They're endangered (especially the groups in the Pacific), facing threats from fishers and boats, plus their eggs are vulnerable on beaches. Their favorite food is jellyfish, making them extra prone to accidentally eating harmful ocean pollution like plastic that looks a lot like their favorite snack.

13

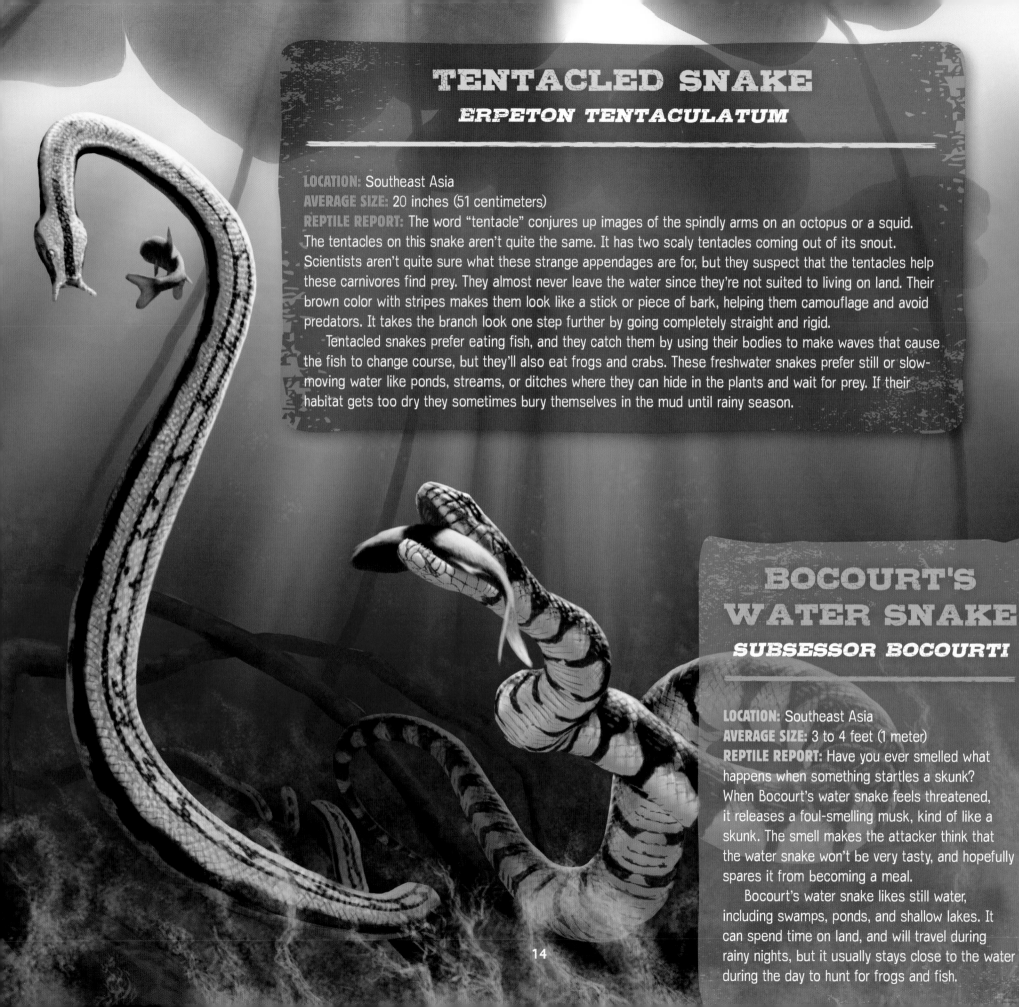

TENTACLED SNAKE
ERPETON TENTACULATUM

LOCATION: Southeast Asia

AVERAGE SIZE: 20 inches (51 centimeters)

REPTILE REPORT: The word "tentacle" conjures up images of the spindly arms on an octopus or a squid. The tentacles on this snake aren't quite the same. It has two scaly tentacles coming out of its snout. Scientists aren't quite sure what these strange appendages are for, but they suspect that the tentacles help these carnivores find prey. They almost never leave the water since they're not suited to living on land. Their brown color with stripes makes them look like a stick or piece of bark, helping them camouflage and avoid predators. It takes the branch look one step further by going completely straight and rigid.

Tentacled snakes prefer eating fish, and they catch them by using their bodies to make waves that cause the fish to change course, but they'll also eat frogs and crabs. These freshwater snakes prefer still or slow-moving water like ponds, streams, or ditches where they can hide in the plants and wait for prey. If their habitat gets too dry they sometimes bury themselves in the mud until rainy season.

BOCOURT'S WATER SNAKE
SUBSESSOR BOCOURTI

LOCATION: Southeast Asia

AVERAGE SIZE: 3 to 4 feet (1 meter)

REPTILE REPORT: Have you ever smelled what happens when something startles a skunk? When Bocourt's water snake feels threatened, it releases a foul-smelling musk, kind of like a skunk. The smell makes the attacker think that the water snake won't be very tasty, and hopefully spares it from becoming a meal.

Bocourt's water snake likes still water, including swamps, ponds, and shallow lakes. It can spend time on land, and will travel during rainy nights, but it usually stays close to the water during the day to hunt for frogs and fish.

YELLOW-BELLIED SEA SNAKE
HYDROPHIS PLATURUS

LOCATION: Indian Ocean and Pacific Ocean
AVERAGE SIZE: 3 to 4 feet (1 meter)
REPTILE REPORT: In cowboy speak, a yellow-bellied person is a coward, but for this snake the term is used quite literally. A vibrant yellow stripe runs along the underside of its body. This saltwater snake is happiest in warm, shallow water, spending hours under the surface without coming up for air. Sometimes, the yellow-bellied sea snake floats along with ocean currents, but it can also swim well and dive down dozens of feet into the water. It's not well-suited to spend time on land. It even has a unique method of breathing in the sea, pulling in oxygen from the water through its skin.

There's a common myth that there are no snakes in Hawaii. That may be true on land, but the yellow-bellied sea snake has been spotted in the water around the islands.

CHRISTMAS MARINE IGUANA
AMBLYRHYNCHUS CRISTATUS VENUSTISSIMUS

LOCATION: Galápagos Islands

AVERAGE SIZE: Males, 4 to 5 feet (1½ meters); females, 2 to 3 feet (¾ meter)

REPTILE REPORT: Nothing screams Christmas like red and green, which is why this brightly colored marine iguana has been nicknamed the Christmas iguana. There are a few different types and colors of marine iguanas in the Galápagos, but the red and green iguanas of Isle Española are undoubtedly the brightest.

   The marine iguana only lives on the volcanic islands of the Galápagos, and it needs access to both the land and the ocean. It lives and sleeps along the coastline or up in mangrove trees, lays its eggs on sandy beaches, and feeds on marine algae that grows in the water. Because the water where it feeds is so cold, it spends lots of time sunbathing to warm itself up again. The water is also very salty, so they have a special gland in their nose that filters it out. Basically, they sneeze out the extra salt.

16

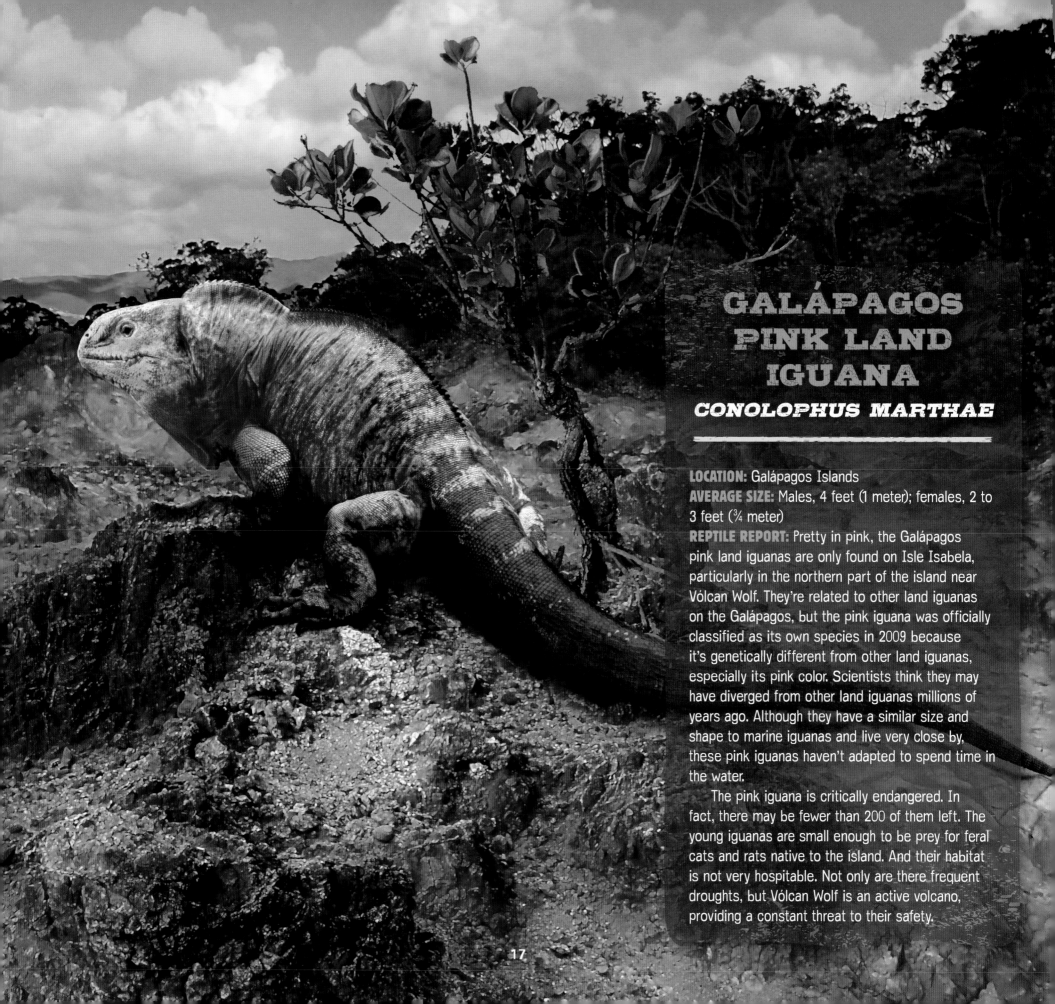

GALÁPAGOS PINK LAND IGUANA
CONOLOPHUS MARTHAE

LOCATION: Galápagos Islands

AVERAGE SIZE: Males, 4 feet (1 meter); females, 2 to 3 feet (¾ meter)

REPTILE REPORT: Pretty in pink, the Galápagos pink land iguanas are only found on Isle Isabela, particularly in the northern part of the island near Vólcan Wolf. They're related to other land iguanas on the Galápagos, but the pink iguana was officially classified as its own species in 2009 because it's genetically different from other land iguanas, especially its pink color. Scientists think they may have diverged from other land iguanas millions of years ago. Although they have a similar size and shape to marine iguanas and live very close by, these pink iguanas haven't adapted to spend time in the water.

The pink iguana is critically endangered. In fact, there may be fewer than 200 of them left. The young iguanas are small enough to be prey for feral cats and rats native to the island. And their habitat is not very hospitable. Not only are there frequent droughts, but Vólcan Wolf is an active volcano, providing a constant threat to their safety.

COMMON FLYING GECKO
PTYCHOZOON KUHLII

LOCATION: Southeast Asia

AVERAGE SIZE: 4 to 7 inches (10 to 17 centimeters)

REPTILE REPORT: It's a bird! It's a plane! It's a…gecko? You might not have expected an airborne reptile, but there are plenty of reptilian species that can spend time in the sky. Despite the name, this one doesn't really fly. It actually glides through the air, using the flaps on the side of its body kind of like a parachute to keep it afloat. It also has webbed feet and a flat tail to aid in gliding. Those flaps also work well as camouflage, allowing this gecko to blend in with trees. They're nocturnal, so during the day they stay motionless, and hidden, on tree trunks. Most nocturnal species don't need a lot of protection from the sun, but because they sleep on trees these geckos are more exposed to the sun's UV rays. Scientists have noticed that they have more skin pigment than other nocturnal species, helping to protect them from the exposure.

Geckos have a unique climbing ability that allows them to cling to just about any surface. Their toe pads have tiny, microscopic hairs that allow them to stick— they can even stick to glass!

BORNEO FLYING SNAKE
CHRYSOPELEA PELIAS

LOCATION: Southeast Asia
AVERAGE SIZE: 2 to 4 feet (1 meter)
REPTILE REPORT: It's hard to imagine anything more frightening than a flying snake. Like other flying reptiles, the Borneo flying snake actually glides through the air. It doesn't have any specialized flaps, but instead it flattens out its body and twists into different shapes to help control its speed and direction as it drifts down from treetops.

The Borneo flying snake is also called the banded flying snake or the twin-barred flying snake because of the markings on its body, and it's one of the more uncommon species of flying snakes. They typically prefer to stay up in the trees, gliding from one to the other and rarely coming all the way down to the ground. They hunt prey from the trees, possibly even using their gliding method not just as a way to travel between trees. They are venomous, using their fangs to stun prey, and although there are some reports of painful bites to humans, there aren't any reported deaths. The venom likely isn't strong enough to do as much damage to a person as it does to the rodents, lizards, birds, bats, and frogs they eat.

BORNEO FLYING DRAGON
DRACO CORNUTUS

LOCATION: Southeast Asia
AVERAGE SIZE: 7 to 8 inches (17 to 20 centimeters)
REPTILE REPORT: You've probably seen a leaf falling from a tree, but what if that leaf was actually a small lizard? The Borneo flying dragon often falls prey to larger animals like flying snakes, so it uses gliding and camouflage to escape and hide. They can flatten their bodies as they glide to help them stay in the air, and their circular shape, along with their green and brown coloring, makes them look almost like a leaf floating through the air. This similarity allows them to stay hidden as they move, deceiving predators into thinking they're just a leaf—nothing to see here!

SANDFISH SKINK

SCINCUS SCINCUS

LOCATION: North Africa and the Arabian Peninsula

AVERAGE SIZE: 6 to 8 inches (15 to 20 centimeters)

REPTILE REPORT: If you've ever been on the beach when a gust of wind hits, you know how hard it is to breathe with sand flying in your face. Well, the sandfish skink spends almost its entire life buried in the sand. Scientists aren't exactly sure how the sandfish skink can breathe when it spends so much time in the sand. They might be able to filter the sand out of their lungs as they breathe in air. The sandfish skink comes out of the sand to look for food, mostly foraging insects like beetles.

Other reptiles regulate their body temperature by moving from the sun to the shade, but the sandfish skink just moves between different layers of sand. The way it moves through the sand is almost like swimming, giving it the name sandfish.

SIDEWINDER
BITIS PERINGUEYI

LOCATION: Namib Desert

AVERAGE SIZE: 8 to 10 inches (20 to 25 centimeters)

REPTILE REPORT: Living in the sand isn't easy, especially in the windy, dune-filled Namib Desert. Slithering forward wouldn't get this snake very far on the unstable ground, so instead it moves by "sidewinding." Instead of going straight, this snake moves to the side, shaping its body into S-shaped curves to navigate the sand.

When the sun in the desert gets too hot, the sidewinder will bury itself in the sand. This is a great way to cool off, and because of this snake's coloring it blends right into the sand, allowing it to wait and ambush its prey.

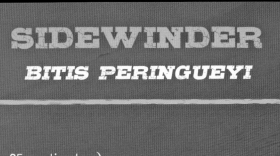

WEB-FOOTED GECKO
PACHYDACTYLUS RANGEI

LOCATION: Namib Desert

AVERAGE SIZE: 4 to 6 inches (10 to 15 centimeters)

REPTILE REPORT: Desert heat doesn't bother this gecko. It's nocturnal, and during the day it burrows into the sand to stay cool. Their large webbed feet help them dig burrows, but they're also an adaptation to help them run across the desert without sinking into the fine sand. Imagine a pair of snowshoes that would help a person stand on the snow without sinking.

Since they hunt at night, they have less competition from other animals when searching out insects like grasshoppers and small spiders. They have large eyes with vertical pupils that help them see in the dark. Their brown and gray coloring helps them blend into their surroundings.

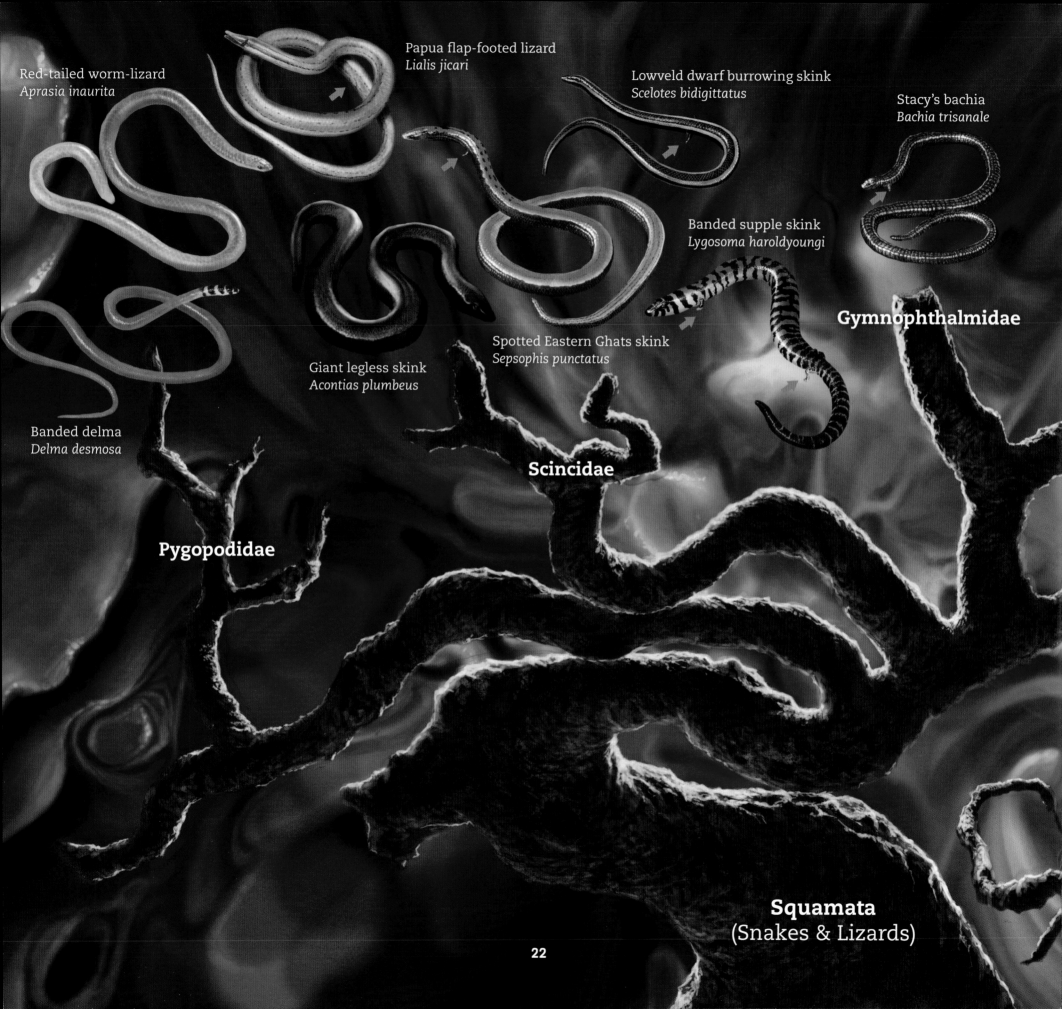

Red-tailed worm-lizard
Aprasia inaurita

Papua flap-footed lizard
Lialis jicari

Lowveld dwarf burrowing skink
Scelotes bidigittatus

Stacy's bachia
Bachia trisanale

Banded supple skink
Lygosoma haroldyoungi

Gymnophthalmidae

Spotted Eastern Ghats skink
Sepsophis punctatus

Giant legless skink
Acontias plumbeus

Banded delma
Delma desmosa

Scincidae

Pygopodidae

Squamata
(Snakes & Lizards)

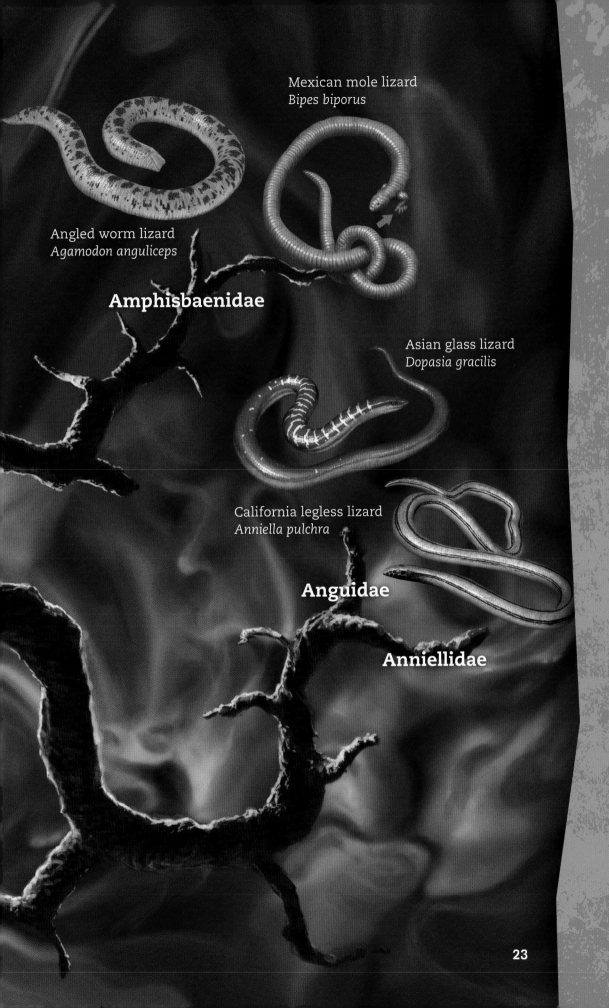

Mexican mole lizard
Bipes biporus

Angled worm lizard
Agamodon anguliceps

Amphisbaenidae

Asian glass lizard
Dopasia gracilis

California legless lizard
Anniella pulchra

Anguidae

Anniellidae

WHO NEEDS LEGS?

It seems like common knowledge: snakes don't have legs. Snakes aren't the only types of reptiles without legs. There are entire families of legless reptiles. The *Amphisbaenidae*, also called worm lizards, are a whole family of legless lizards that look kind of like earthworms. Then there's the *Anguinae*. Although there are some species in this family that look just like snakes, they're actually legless lizards. And the *Pygopodidae* are a type of gecko without legs—they look kind of like snakes, but they don't have the classic forked tongue. Some types of lizards, like the *Gymnophthalmidae* and the *Scincidae*, have legs, but they're very short and aren't very helpful.

But the bigger scientific question is *why* don't some reptiles have legs? To answer this question we have to go back millions of years. Evolutionary evidence tells us that many of these reptiles' ancestors used to have legs about 150 million years ago. But when some reptiles adapted from walking to slithering, their genetics changed, too. As many species adapted to burrowing and used their legs less and less, their DNA changed. That's why some reptiles still have shortened legs or claws, while others have fully adapted DNA. Some snakes, especially pythons, show evidence that their ancestors used to have legs. They have bumps on the sides of their pelvis that indicate where legs would go—their DNA just doesn't tell them to grow legs when they're born.

Because their bodies still sometimes retain the structure to support legs, it's possible that legless reptiles could eventually evolve further and redevelop legs. But in general, it seems that most legless reptiles don't have legs because they didn't need them.

CHAPTER 2

DRAGONS ALIVE

Dragons in myths and legends are often flying, fearsome, fire-breathing giants. Those types of dragons are just the stuff of stories. There are no giant, winged, horned lizards hiding out in forest caves (or guarding princesses locked in towers).

But most stories have a grain of truth somewhere in them, and the legendary dragons are no exception. In reality, there are plenty of reptiles with characteristics that could have inspired the stories. There are massive reptiles that can grow to be 10-feet long, there are predator reptiles with terrifying teeth, and there are plenty of scaly, spiky creatures hidden away in nature that resemble real-life versions of mythical dragons.

BORNEO EARLESS MONITOR
LANTHANOTUS BORNEENSIS

LOCATION: Borneo
AVERAGE SIZE: 1 to 2 feet (½ meter)
REPTILE REPORT: Monitor lizards are a modern-day reminder of reptiles' dinosaur ancestors. This family of lizards has long necks, powerful limbs and claws, and thick tails. Monitor lizards are carnivores, and are well adapted to being fierce predators. The Borneo earless monitor has the appearance of being earless, but that doesn't mean it can't hear. Their smooth heads have an ear opening that allows them to hear even though they don't have visible ears.

The Borneo earless monitor is a nocturnal, semiaquatic lizard. That means it's active during the daytime, and it can spend time both on land and in the water. During the day, they burrow in the ground (usually near water). This inactive lizard may seem lazy because it can stand completely motionless underwater for hours, just lifting its nose to breathe. But this lizard is actually hunting, waiting for the fish and crustaceans it likes to eat. Once they get close enough, it pounces with quick spurts of speed and powerful jaws. They can even swallow their prey while they're underwater. Its powerful tail is prehensile, which means it can wrap around stones and branches, allowing it to hold on in powerful currents without being swept away.

GIANT MONITOR LIZARD
MEGALANIA PRISCA

LOCATION: Australia

AVERAGE SIZE: 16 to 23 feet (4 to 7 meters)

REPTILE REPORT: Did you know that a standard minivan is around 16 feet long? Next time you see a minivan driving down the road, imagine that it's actually a giant lizard. That's about how big the giant monitor lizard was. Unfortunately, this prehistoric lizard went extinct about 50,000 years ago, and scientists have only been able to study it from fossils. They don't even have a complete skeleton, so they're guessing at just how big this monstrous lizard was, but they do know it was one of the largest lizards to ever walk on land. Today, the Komodo dragon of Indonesia is the largest living land lizard, measuring about 10 feet long. Early humans in Australia would have been around at the same time as the giant monitor lizards, and the people probably encountered these massive creatures as they settled the land. Scientists think that these early humans might have been part of the reason this lizard went extinct, since there was growing competition for land and food.

The giant monitor lizard would have lived in forests or open woodlands, and scientists have even found some fossils in rivers and caves. This predator would have been top of the food chain, and, based on fossils found nearby, it likely ate large mammals or reptiles, including animals similar to kangaroos.

DRAGON SNAKE

XENODERMUS JAVANICUS

LOCATION: Southeast Asia

AVERAGE SIZE: 2 to 3 feet (¾ meter)

REPTILE REPORT: This nocturnal snake is incredibly mysterious. It's most commonly found on the island of Java. During the day it burrows in the mud near water or streams, hunting exclusively at night for frogs, tadpoles, and fish. Most snakes have smooth skin, but the dragon snake has three rows of raised scales running down its back. Part of why this snake is so mysterious is because it doesn't like to be approached. When it feels threatened, it will stiffen up its whole body.

AFRICAN HAIRY BUSH VIPER

ATHERIS HISPIDA

LOCATION: Africa

AVERAGE SIZE: 1½ to 2 feet (½ meter)

REPTILE REPORT: A hairy snake? It's not real hair, but the African hairy bush viper's unique scales give this snake its name. They're raised and pointed, giving the snake a bristly, hairy appearance. This rainforest-dwelling snake likes a habitat with both trees and water sources like swamps. It's nocturnal, and during the day it's usually coiled up, elevated in bushes and small trees. It comes down to the ground to hunt, usually eating small mammals and frogs.

Vipers are a family of venomous snakes most well-known for their long, pointed fangs. Those fangs are hinged, and when the snake isn't using them the fangs fold up in its mouth, almost disappearing.

GIANT GIRDLED LIZARD
SMAUG GIGANTEUS

LOCATION: South Africa

AVERAGE SIZE: 1 to 1½ feet (¼ meter)

REPTILE REPORT: If you've ever read *The Hobbit*, you'll probably recognize the name Smaug, the dragon that Bilbo Baggins encounters. In the book, Smaug was a heavily armored dragon who lived underground. The real-life *Smaug giganteus* shares quite a few similarities with the character. Its body is covered with pointed, spiny scales that work as a type of armor to protect it from predators. They live in burrows (sometimes sharing the burrow with other lizards of the same species) and rarely stray far from their home. If they feel threatened, they'll sometimes go partially into the burrow, leaving their armored tail exposed and swinging it around to deter intruders.

This lizard is part of a family of girdled lizards, and it's sometimes called a sungazer lizard because it likes to rest staring up toward the sun. Although it's not giant compared to some other reptiles, it is the largest of the girdled lizards.

RED-EYED CROCODILE SKINK
TRIBOLONOTUS GRACILIS

LOCATION: Papua New Guinea and the Admiralty Islands

AVERAGE SIZE: 6 to 8 inches (15 to 20 centimeters)

REPTILE REPORT: Can you imagine anything more bone-chilling than a pair of red eyes looking at you? The red-eyed crocodile skink is named for its two most prominent features. Its eyes themselves aren't red (the pupils are more dark brown), but the scales around its eyes can be orange or red in color. And as for the crocodile part of this animal's name, it has four rows of scales that look very similar to crocodile scales. Young red-eyed crocodile skinks don't have those characteristic red eyes. The color doesn't develop until they're about 6 months old.

These forest-dwelling lizards like to be near water, where they can nest under forest debris and soil. Red-eyed crocodile skinks are often found on coconut plantations.

ANAIMALAI SPINY LIZARD

SALEA ANAMALLAYANA

LOCATION: India

AVERAGE SIZE: 10 to 12 inches (25 to 30 centimeters)

REPTILE REPORT: With a row of tall, pointed spines along its back, this interesting lizard looks like it has a mohawk. The Anaimalai spiny lizard lives in mountain forests, specifically in the Anaimalai Hills of India. Its body coloring allows it to blend in well with trees, and when threatened it will keep still to avoid being noticed.

These slow-moving lizards usually eat insects. Their tails are usually longer than their entire bodies.

PHUKET HORNED TREE AGAMID

ACANTHOSAURA PHUKETENSIS

LOCATION: Thailand

AVERAGE SIZE: 8 to 12 inches (20 to 30 centimeters)

REPTILE REPORT: Phuket, one of the islands of Thailand, is home to some of the most beautiful nature in the world, with its stunning beaches and soaring mountains. The Phuket horned tree agamid lives hidden in the forests of the island's mountainous region. These lizards feed on insects and the occasional fish and live in just that small region of Thailand, so one of their biggest threats is the deforestation of Phuket.

This species was only discovered a few years ago, so scientists still have a lot to learn about it. With the long, hornlike spines on their head and down their back, it's easy to see where this lizard got its name.

SMOOTH-FRONTED CAIMAN
PALEOSUCHUS TRIGONATUS

LOCATION: South America

AVERAGE SIZE: 5 to 7 feet (1½ to 2 meters)

REPTILE REPORT: You've probably heard of crocodiles and alligators, but did you know that in South America they have a close relative called the caiman? Caimans live in streams and rivers, and the smooth-fronted caiman has been found in the Amazon River and the Orinoco River. Many caiman species have a ridge on their head, but the smooth-fronted caiman doesn't, making this species easy to distinguish from its relatives (and explaining its nickname). It's also noticeably smaller than other crocodilian reptiles. The caiman can hunt both in the water and on land. Younger caiman will usually eat fish, reptiles, and aquatic insects. Adult caimans usually move to the forest, looking for larger prey like porcupines and pacas.

Female caimans will sometimes build their nests close to termite mounds because the termite nests generate heat that help incubate caiman eggs.

ALLIGATOR SNAPPING TURTLE
MACROCHELYS TEMMINCKII

LOCATION: Southeastern United States

AVERAGE SIZE: 2½ to 3 feet (¾ meter)

REPTILE REPORT: With its large size, powerful jaws, and tall ridges on its shell, the alligator snapping turtle looks a lot like Bowser from the Super Mario games. These turtles are the largest freshwater species, weighing in at nearly 200 pounds (90 kilograms), and they like to live in large bodies of deep water, like rivers, lakes, or swamps. Strong jaws are common to all snapping turtles, but unlike smaller common snapping turtles, the alligator snapping turtle has eyes on the side of its head rather than on top. They typically live for more than 20 years in the wild, and they spend most of that time in the water. They can stay motionless and nearly invisible under the water for more than 40 minutes, only coming up to the surface for air.

If you've ever gone fishing, you know it's important to lure in fish. That's just how a snapping turtle hunts—by patiently hiding in the murky water with its mouth open. In contrast to the rest of its gray body and mouth, its tongue is pink, which makes it look a little like a worm, which attracts fish. That's where the snapping part of its name comes in. Once the fish get close enough, the turtle snaps its jaws shut, trapping the fish and often swallowing it whole. It will also eat mollusks, insects, and other small reptiles.

That powerful bite certainly could be dangerous to a human that gets too close. A snapping turtle won't often attack a human unprovoked, but if it feels threatened it's likely to snap its jaws shut.

This forest-dwelling lizard has a row of spines down its back and a large pouch of skin on its neck. It clings to tree branches and, rather than hunting actively, waits for insects to come to it.

CROWNED FOREST DRAGON
LOPHOSAURUS DILOPHUS

LOCATION: Indonesia and New Guinea
AVERAGE SIZE: 1½ to 2 feet (½ meter)
REPTILE REPORT: If you use your imagination, the ridges on top of this lizard's head look like a crown that a king might wear. The crowned forest dragon is mostly beige or green in color, but when it opens its mouth, it reveals a bright yellow tongue.

PINOCCHIO LIZARD
ANOLIS PROBOSCIS

LOCATION: Ecuador
AVERAGE SIZE: 9 to 11 inches (22 to 27 centimeters)
REPTILE REPORT: In the story of Pinocchio, Pinocchio's nose grows every time he tells a lie. If that's true, then the Pinocchio lizard has told a lot of lies, because the horn on its snout measures about three-quarters of an inch. This rare lizard has fascinated scientists for years. It was first described in 1956, but then nobody spotted another one for about 40 years. It was rediscovered in 2005 by bird-watchers.

Only the males have the characteristic horn, and scientists aren't quite sure why, but even male hatchlings have a small horn. Their color helps them to camouflage with the trees, and they move very, very slowly, making them very difficult to see. Maybe that's why it took so long for them to be rediscovered.

34

MONA ISLAND IGUANA
CYCLURA STEJNEGERI

LOCATION: Puerto Rico
AVERAGE SIZE: 3 to 4 feet (¾ to 1 meter)
REPTILE REPORT: Sometimes called the rhinoceros lizard, the Mona Island Iguana is a land-dwelling lizard with a horn-like spine on its snout. It eats mostly fruit, flowers, and leaves (and sometimes crabs or insects) in its dry, rocky habitat, and it hides in caves or rocky areas to cool off. It's the largest lizard in Puerto Rico, and its tail makes up about half of its overall body length. Because they live off native plants, they are threatened by other more competitive animals fighting for the same resources, especially goats and pigs. The species is considered endangered, making it even more important to protect their natural habitat on Mona Island.

USAMBARA THREE-HORNED CHAMELEON
TRIOCEROS DEREMENSIS

LOCATION: Tanzania
AVERAGE SIZE: 12 to 16 inches (30 to 40 centimeters)
REPTILE REPORT: If you could miniaturize a *Triceratops*, it might look a lot like the Usambara three-horned chameleon. This rainforest lizard has three distinctive horns on its face that look an awful lot like the ancient dinosaur.

You may have heard that chameleons can change colors to match just about any surrounding. While they can't make just any color or pattern appear on their skin, chameleons do have a unique ability to adapt their skin color. Usambara three-horned chameleons are typically green with yellowish or off-white markings to camouflage with their surroundings, but when they're excited or stressed they sometimes show spots of green or black on their bodies.

Chameleons have one of the most unique feeding methods, shooting out their incredibly long tongues to catch insects midair and pull them in.

FOREST DRAGON
CORYTOPHANES CRISTATUS

LOCATION: Central America
AVERAGE SIZE: 12 to 16 inches (30 to 40 centimeters)
REPTILE REPORT: When you ride your bike, you probably wear a helmet to protect your head. Well, the forest dragon wears a helmet, too! Sometimes, the forest dragon is called a helmeted iguana because it has a raised, helmet-like crest on the top of its head. They live in tropical rainforests, usually in bushes or low trees, and eat insects as well as worms and smaller lizards. The forest dragon is usually brown or gray with some red or green markings. Like some other lizards, they can adapt the color of their skin to help them camouflage, and if they feel threatened they'll completely freeze to avoid being seen. But, if freezing fails and there's still a threat, they can expand the crest on their head, along with a pouch on their neck, to make themselves look bigger.

Their ability to keep as still as a statue isn't just for when they feel threatened. They rarely move much, and in the wild some of these lizards have been spotted with moss or other small plants growing on top of their head, showing just how inactive they are.

WATER DRAGON
HYDROSAURUS PUSTULATUS

LOCATION: Philippines

AVERAGE SIZE: 2 to 3 feet (¾ meter)

REPTILE REPORT: Sailboats move because their sails trap wind and push the boat forward. Water dragons don't need a boat—they have sails right on their backs. The "sails" are actually stiff skin that can stand as tall as 2 or 3 inches. Only males have the sail, and scientist aren't exactly sure what purpose it serves. It could be all about display, helping them defend their territory or find a mate, or it could be to help them regulate their temperature. Having more exposed skin could help them warm up and cool down more quickly.

Water dragons live near rivers and streams in tropical jungles, and they're excellent swimmers. These omnivores eat mostly leaves and fruit, along with some insects and crustaceans. If threatened, they'll jump in the water and swim to the bottom to get out of danger. They have flattened toes, kind of like flippers, that make them good swimmers. Young, light lizards can even use those toes to run across the surface of the water.

CHAPTER 3

HIDE AND SEEK

The rules of hide and seek are easy. Pick a spot to hide where nobody can find you. In the wild, there are plenty of places to hide, from treetops to the deepest burrows. And animals know all of the best places to hide from predators. But there are lots of animals that take it one step further. They don't just hide, they hide in plain sight. Camouflage gives animals a unique way to blend in with their surroundings so they're always hidden. Their colors and patterns help them to almost disappear into their surroundings, making it much harder to spot them.

There are a few reasons why animals don't want to be seen. The first is for protection. If a predator can't see you, it can't hurt you. Smaller animals stay safe when they blend in with their environment. Hunters use camouflage, too. Instead of looking dangerous, which would alert prey and scare them off, these animals hide in their habitat, then pounce before the prey even knows what got them.

MATA MATA
CHELUS FIMBRIATA

LOCATION: South America

AVERAGE SIZE: 18 to 20 inches (45 to 50 centimeters)

REPTILE REPORT: With a name like mata mata, it's no surprise this turtle is a fierce hunter—*mata, mata* means "kill, kill" in Spanish—but its hunting prowess doesn't come from speed or force. Instead, the mata mata is exceptionally patient, with an amazing ability to hide without being noticed. The mata mata inhabits slow-moving, muddy, shallow water, like swamps, marshes, and streams, and it blends right into its surroundings. Its gray, brownish coloring makes it look like a pile of muddy debris, and its ridged shell is sometimes covered in algae, helping it blend in even more. It has flaps of skin along its head and neck that move slightly with changes in the current, much like vegetation or plants would. They rarely move or leave the water, and their snouts have developed into a long, protruding nose that can be used like a snorkel to breathe without needing to come all the way up to the surface.

So what exactly is it waiting for with all that camouflage? The mata mata eats fish and other small aquatic animals, swallowing them whole.

EVOLUTIONARY ADAPTATIONS

If you looked at the tree and the bark moved, you might think you were imagining things. Tree bark isn't supposed to move, of course, but there are a lot of reptiles that make themselves look like bark so that they can blend into the trunks of trees. There are even reptiles that look like the leaves of trees and bushes, so they almost disappear when they're sitting on a branch. For forest-dwelling reptiles, looking like the foliage is key to blending in and staying safe from predators.

The leaf-tailed gecko (*Uroplatus*) is one family that likes to look like a leaf. There are a few types of leaf-tailed geckos, and they use different types of camouflage that make them very difficult to see, like the mossy leaf-tailed gecko (*Uroplatus sikorae*). Larger geckos in this family have brown or green markings so they look like moss or bark.

Some of the smaller members of this family have ridges on their body that look like the veins of a leaf.

Chameleons are very well known for their camouflage abilities—they can actually change colors. Species like the veiled chameleon (*Chamaeleo calyptratus calcarife*) and the graceful chameleon (*Chamaeleo gracilis gracilis*) are normally green in color, but they can change their colors from a range of green to brown to yellow. There are a few reasons why they change. Sometimes, it's to better blend in, but it can also be a sign of stress, mating, or defending their territory. Beyond just their coloring, species like the Antimena chameleon (*Furcifer antimena*) and the West Usambara two-horned chameleon (*Kinyongia multituberculata*) also have spines and markings that help them appear more leaf-like.

THAT HELP REPTILES BLEND IN WITH FOLIAGE AND BARK WHEN LIVING IN TREES AND BUSHES

The camouflage can go beyond just markings. Flying lizards (*Draco ornatus*) have flaps on the sides of their body that they can spread out and use to glide through the air. The wide, rounded shape makes these lizards look like a leaf falling through the air, keeping them hidden even when they're on the move.

Small lizards are more vulnerable to predators, but what they lack in size they make up for in camouflage. The Auckland green gecko (*Naultinus elegans*), for example, is mostly green with some white and brown markings to help it blend into the trees. Geckos have feet that are especially well-adapted to climbing, so being hidden in the leaves is a big advantage. Size can actually help these reptiles. When paired with the right coloring, they virtually disappear, like the pygmy chameleon

(*Rhampholeon acuminatus*). And some larger species try to make themselves look smaller than they actually are, like the Cat gecko (*Aeluroscalabotes felinus*), which curls its body up into a tight circle to sleep like a cat does.

Lizards aren't the only reptiles that blend in with the trees. There are plenty of arboreal (tree-dwelling) snakes, and they rely on blending into the trees both for protection and for hunting. Some look like the branches, like the South African twig snake (*Thelotornis capensis*), which has a brown body and white markings that make it look just like a twig. This snake is an ambush predator. It hides and waits for its prey, then pounces. Some members of the *Siphlophis* snake family have similar striped markings in greens, browns, and yellows.

South African twig snake
Thelotornis capensis

Veiled chameleon
Chamaeleo calyptratus

Cat gecko
Aeluroscalabotes felinus

Mossy leaf-tailed gecko
Uroplatus sikorae

Meller's chameleon
Trioceros melleri

Graceful chameleon
Chamaeleo gracilis

Auckland green gecko
Naultinus elegans

46

Worontzow's Spotted Night Snake
Siphlophis worontzowi

West Usambara two-horned chamaeleon
Kinyongia multituberculata

White-spotted flying dragon
Draco ornatus

Antimena chameleon
Furcifer antimena

EVOLUTIONARY ADAPTATIONS

What's on the floor of your bedroom right now? If you haven't cleaned up in a little while, there might be toys or clothes or books on the floor. The same is true on the forest floor. There are rocks and branches and leaves littered across it. So when they're on the ground, it helps reptiles blend in so they look like just another piece of clutter.

Fallen leaves make up a big part of the ground covering, so a leaf-like pattern makes for great camouflage. Some species adapt these markings to hide from predators, like the zomba pygmy chameleon (*Rieppeleon brachyurus*) with leaf-like veins and a brown color that makes them look like a dead leaf that's fallen to the ground. The Western leaf lizard (*Stenocercus fimbriatus*) also does a great impression of a dead leaf. Not only do they have the right coloring and markings to look like a dead leaf, but they also sit perfectly still when they're threatened so that they blend right in.

Some of these reptiles look a little ridiculous when they're out of their element. Some of them have intricate patterns, like the Borneo short-tailed python (*Python breitensteini*) or the Gaboon viper (*Bitis gabonica*). Those patterns seem bold when the snake is against a plain background, but they perfectly match the pattern of the leaves and sticks on the forest floor. That's because the forest floor is patterned with plants, leaves, sticks, and rocks. Having a pattern of different colors and markings helps reptiles blend in.

THAT HELP REPTILES BLEND IN WITH THE FOREST FLOOR

Ruida's Anole (*Anolis megalopithecus*) is able to hide in the open among grass, twigs, and dirt thanks to its coloring of brown, green, or beige markings.

Some reptiles like to play in the mud, and having brown markings can help them camouflage better on the muddy ground. The rainforest-dwelling Central American bushmaster (*Lachesis stenophrys*) has a glossy brown, scaly body that makes it look almost like it's covered in mud. And a pattern of brown, black, and green markings help the Mexican musk turtle (*Staurotypus triporcatus*) match the muddy, sandy colors of its watery habitat.

HOW MANY REPTILES CAN YOU FIND IN THIS SCENE?

50

Central American bushmaster
Lachesis stenophrys

Mexican giant musk turtle
Staurotypus triporcatus

Borneo short-tailed python
Python breitensteini

52

Ruida's anole
Anole megalopithecus

Gaboon viper
Bitis gabonica

Western leaf lizard
Stenocercus fimbriatus

Beardless pygmy chameleon
Rieppeleon brachyurus

53

EVOLUTIONARY ADAPTATIONS

In the forest, there are lots of places to hide in the leaves or branches, but in sandy, rocky desert environments it's much harder to find a hiding place. Reptiles have to adapt in lots of unique ways to live in deserts, from moving differently on the sandy, rocky ground to adapting to survive in warmer temperatures. Reptiles in the desert burrow into the ground, so matching the environment helps them stay concealed even though there aren't branches or leaves to cover them up.

Rocks can be textured or pebbly, so having a patterned black, gray, and white body can help to create the illusion of blending into a rocky terrain. That's what the spiny-tailed lizard (*Uromastyx yemenensis*) and the golden spiny-tailed gecko (*Strophurus taenicauda*) do to survive. They have a patterned body that matches the rocky surface. There are lots of similar lizards that have patterns and markings to look like rocks—the climber lizard (*Phymaturus spurcus*) has a similar pattern.

Grasslands don't offer much coverage, making it difficult for both predators and prey to hide. Camouflage is some of the best protection, keeping reptiles concealed even when they're out in the open. To blend into the beige sand and grass in its habitat, the plain mountain adder (*Bitis inornata*) is colored a sandy reddish-beige. But the ground isn't always just one color. Sometimes it's made up of sand, rocks, and grasses, like the environment where the West Indian leopard gecko (*Eublepharis fuscus*) lives. Its patterned body has a combination of colors, spots, and stripes that helps it to blend in with the different surfaces and textures.

THAT HELP REPTILES BLEND IN WITH ROCKS AND SAND

Desert sand is some of the hardest terrain to blend into, especially in the red sand deserts of western Australia. With a combination of red and beige markings on its body, the helmeted gecko (*Diplodactylus galeatus*) is able to easily blend into the unique sand in Australia. The Gibber earless dragon (*Tympanocryptis intima*) has adapted to blend into the desert as well, with its red and beige patterned body. Australia is also home to the crested dragon (*Ctenophorus cristatus*). Its brown, beige, and reddish markings—including its striped tail—help it blend into the ground.

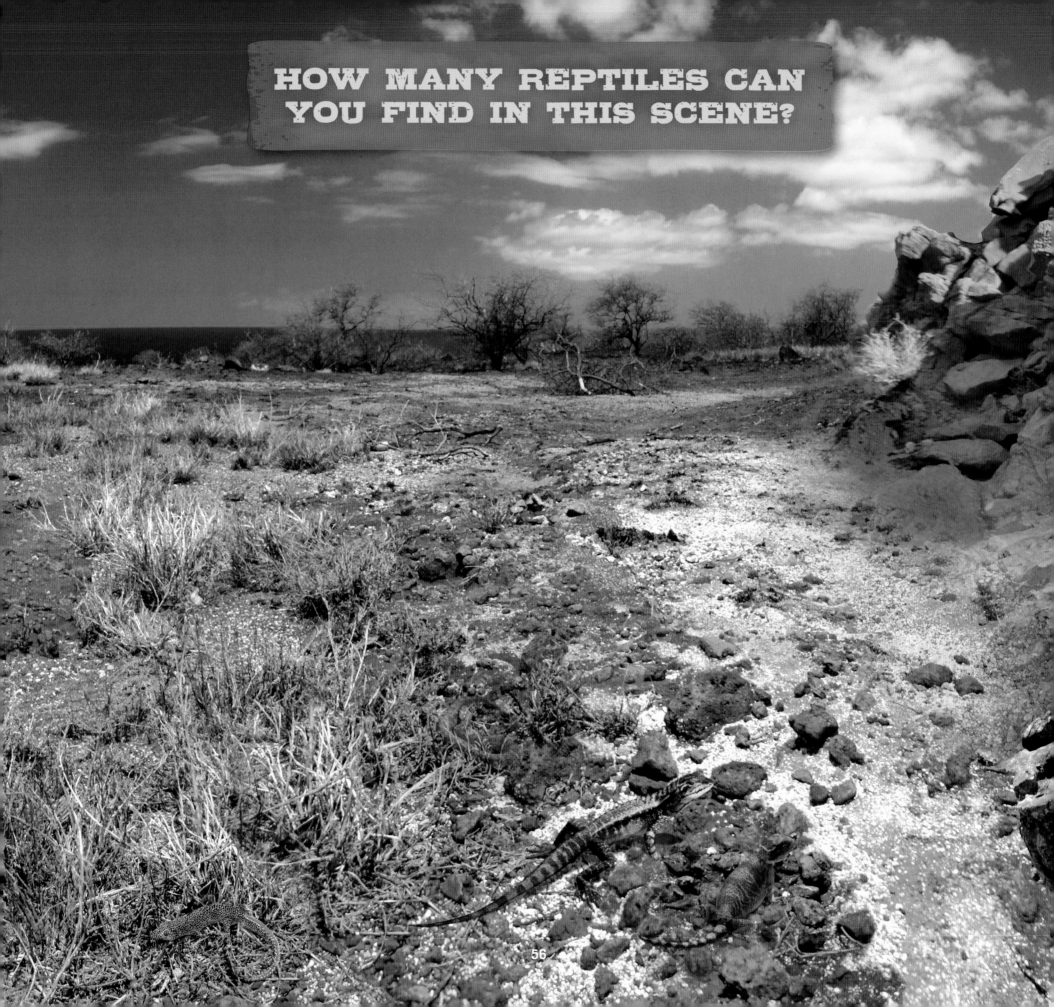

Plain mountain adder
Bitis inornata

Crested dragon
Ctenophorus cristatus

Golden spiny-tailed gecko
Strophurus taenicauda

Gibber earless dragon
Tympanocryptis intima

Climber lizard
Phymaturus spurcus

South Arabian spiny-tailed lizard
Uromastyx yemenensis

Helmeted gecko
Diplodactylus galeatus

West Indian leopard gecko
Eublepharis fuscus

59

CHAPTER 4

DRAMATIC DISPLAYS, DEFENSES, AND SUPERPOWERS

There's a saying that nature is a "survival of the fittest" battle, but fittest doesn't always mean biggest. Size certainly helps, but there are plenty of other ways for animals to protect themselves from danger.

From spitting blood to injecting venom, reptiles have some incredibly creative defensive tactics. They've found ways to make themselves look much bigger and more intimidating than they are, like the secret toad-headed agama (see page 64) and the frilled lizard (see page 66). Or they'll make noise to scare off threats, like the eastern diamondback rattlesnake (see page 68). Some even show how threatening they are with their colors, like the eastern coral snake (see page 76).

The species that don't have the best defenses go with a "fake it till you make it" approach. These species sometimes pretend to be a more dangerous species. Sometimes, the attacker is confused or intimidated enough to just leave them alone.

BLUE-TONGUED SKINK
TILIQUA MULTIFASCIATA

LOCATION: Australia

AVERAGE SIZE: 15 to 18 inches (38 to 45 centimeters)

REPTILE REPORT: Have you ever eaten a piece of candy that turned your tongue neon? That's what the blue-tongued skink's tongue looks like. It doesn't eat candy, though. Instead, it eats mostly seeds, insects, and other items it forages from the ground. The tongue isn't blue because of what it eats. It's actually a way to scare off predators. When threatened, it sticks out its tongue. The vibrant color reflects back UV rays and can momentarily stun an approaching predator.

Its tongue is bright, but the rest of its body is a more subtly colored brown or beige with orange markings and a black stripe near its eyes. It has short, small limbs. Although many reptiles lay eggs, the blue-tongued skink is viviparous, which means it gives birth to live young.

SECRET TOAD-HEADED AGAMA
PHRYNOCEPHALUS MYSTACEUS

LOCATION: Middle East
AVERAGE SIZE: 9 to 10 inches (22 to 25 centimeters)
REPTILE REPORT: This lizard is unassuming at first glance, but it's hiding a secret. The secret toad-headed lizard has frills on the sides of its head that are bright pink or red. The frills are usually tucked away, but when their territory is threatened or a predator approaches, this lizard fans its frills out to the side to make itself look bigger and shakes its tail like a scorpion would to show dominance. They live on the ground in sand dunes, burrowing into the sand for shelter or to cool off.

SUPERB LARGE FAN-THROATED LIZARD
SARADA SUPERBA

LOCATION: India

AVERAGE SIZE: 8 to 10 inches (20 to 25 centimeters)

REPTILE REPORT: Fan-throated lizards have a brightly colored flap of skin on their throat that looks like a foldable paper fan. The flap, called a dewlap, seems to be mostly used to attract mates and to intimidate mating competitors. It's beautiful to look at, and only male lizards have the flap. It's an iridescent blue with some orange and black in it, and the name superb refers to its vibrant, superb colors. Females have a small flap under their throat, but it's typically just white in color.

They live in hot, dry areas where they perch on or near rocks, and when the ground gets too hot they'll sometimes stand up and walk on just their hind legs.

FRILLED LIZARD
CHLAMYDOSAURUS KINGII

LOCATION: Australia and New Guinea
AVERAGE SIZE: 3 feet (1 meter)
REPTILE REPORT: When the frilled lizard is threatened, it looks like something right out of *Jurassic Park*. The colorful, pleated flap of skin around its neck (called a frill) expands to make the lizard look larger. The frill is usually yellow or orange, and when the lizard opens its frill it usually hisses and stands up on its hind legs.

So what does it do if the attacker doesn't back down? If the display doesn't make the predator leave it alone, the frilled lizard turns and runs for a tree as fast as it can—with the frill still open.

The frilled lizard lives in the forests of Australia, and spends most of its time up in trees, eating spiders, insects, and small mammals. If they do come down from the trees, it's usually only to hunt. When their frill isn't expanded, it rests over their shoulders, almost like a cape.

BUTTERFLY LIZARD
LEIOLEPIS BELLIANA

LOCATION: Southeast Asia
AVERAGE SIZE: 15 to 16 inches (38 to 40 centimeters)
REPTILE REPORT: Picture a monarch butterfly with its iconic orange and black markings. The butterfly lizard gets its name from the flaps on its sides with a pattern of orange and black marks that look a lot like the monarch. Other than the markings on its sides, the butterfly lizard is mostly gray or green in color with spots running down its back.

These burrowing lizards often live in sandy areas (they're sometimes found hiding at golf courses), and they'll run back to their burrow if they feel threatened. They mostly eat insects, along with some plants. Although they're not native to the United States, there have been some reports of butterfly lizards spotted in Florida. The butterfly lizard is sometimes sold as a pet, which could be how they end up so far from their natural habitat.

EASTERN DIAMONDBACK RATTLESNAKE
CROTALUS ADAMANTEUS

LOCATION: Southeastern United States
AVERAGE SIZE: 4 to 6 feet (1 to 2 meters)
REPTILE REPORT: Rattlesnakes are some of the most recognizable snakes, thanks to being fixtures in movies and TV shows for their dangerous bite and audible rattle. That noise comes from them rapidly moving their rattle-like tail tip. The rattle portion itself is made up of loosely attached, hollow segments. If the snake senses danger it makes the rattling noise to intimidate and scare away the threat. But these snakes don't always use the rattle before attacking. If they're hunting prey and want to pounce undetected, they won't make any noise at all.

The eastern diamondback rattlesnake is one of the most recognizable and one of the largest types of rattlesnake. The scales on its body are usually dark green, brown, or black, and it has a pattern of diamond shapes down its back with yellow or tan scales. Their beautiful markings can actually be what kills them—people hunt diamondbacks for their prized skin. Diamondbacks typically like dry, grassy or sandy areas, and although they don't usually live near the water they will sometimes live in swampy areas or coastal sand dunes.

Rattlesnakes are vipers, which means they have venomous fangs that fold back when they're not in use. They hunt small rodents and birds, as well as some larger prey like rabbits. Their venom can kill a person if a bite is left untreated, but luckily treatments do exist that can save a bite victim.

MIMIC GLASS LIZARD
OPHISAURUS MIMICUS

LOCATION: Southeastern United States

AVERAGE SIZE: 15 to 25 inches (38 to 63 centimeters)

REPTILE REPORT: If you've ever dropped a piece of glass, you know that it breaks very easily. The same is true of the mimic glass lizard. When it's grabbed, the lizard's tail will break off. Their tail makes up about half of their length, and the predator that grabbed it is usually distracted by the tail breaking off, giving the lizard a chance to escape. Don't worry, the tail grows back.

Although it looks like a snake, the mimic glass lizard is actually a legless lizard. They live in dry, warm areas and eat insects and spiders.

PHILIPPINE PIT VIPER
TRIMERESURUS FLAVOMACULATUS

LOCATION: Philippines

AVERAGE SIZE: 1 to 1½ feet (½ meter)

REPTILE REPORT: The name pit viper might have you thinking this snake lives in a pit, but that's not the case. The "pit" actually refers to the pit organs on the snake's face. The pit organs allow the viper to sense heat, and because they hunt small, warm-blooded mammals and birds (along with some lizards and frogs), they can often sense their prey before they can even see it thanks to the heat-sensing pit organs.

There are a few different species of pits vipers around the world. The Philippine pit viper lives only in the forests of the Philippines, and it has unique green coloring with reddish-brown markings.

BEADED LIZARD
HELODERMA HORRIDUM

LOCATION: Mexico

AVERAGE SIZE: 2 to 3 feet (¾ meter)

REPTILE REPORT: This lizard has a hidden superpower. It's one of the only known venomous lizards. That venom does double duty. It helps catch prey (small mammals, birds, and other lizards), which it swallows whole. But the venom is also a defense mechanism, stunning or paralyzing predators and giving the beaded lizard time to escape.

The name beaded lizard comes from the strong, bead-like scales covering their body. They have a long, thick tail that has the ability to store extra fat, which can help keep the lizard alive if food becomes scarce.

COLLETT'S SNAKE
PSEUDECHIS COLLETTI

LOCATION: Australia

AVERAGE SIZE: 5 to 6 feet (1½ meters)

REPTILE REPORT: Think about how air releases out of a balloon as it deflates. The balloon flattens, and the escaping air lets out a hissing noise. That's kind of what Collett's snake does to scare away predators. When it feels like it's in danger, the snake inflates its body and lifts up, and then it lets out a hissing noise as its neck flattens to the side to make its head look larger. If that intimidation tactic fails, this snake has a backup plan. A threatened Collett's snake will bite, injecting the predator with toxic venom.

Collett's snake is beautifully colored, with bands of pattern that range in color from cream to pink to orange to red to brown. It likes dry, flat plains and eats lizards, small mammals, and frogs.

TIGER RATSNAKE
SPILOTES PULLATUS

LOCATION: Central and South America
AVERAGE SIZE: 7 to 8 feet (2 meters)
REPTILE REPORT: The tiger ratsnake is nonvenomous, but that doesn't mean it won't try to scare off threats. Instead of venom, it has the ability to make its neck look larger to intimidate predators, and it has a quick, powerful strike. They prefer to live in forests near a coast or close to the water since they spend most of their time in trees.

The name tiger comes from the bold black and yellow markings on its body. And the second part of its name refers to its diet. Ratsnakes will eat rodents, small mammals, birds, lizards, frogs, and just about anything else they can catch.

ZEBRA SPITTING COBRA
NAJA NIGRICINCTA

LOCATION: Namibia and Angola
AVERAGE SIZE: 4 to 5 feet (1 to 1½ meters)
REPTILE REPORT: Did you know that llamas spit if they're angry? The zebra spitting cobra takes the same approach, and kicks it up a notch. If it's in danger, this snake spits venom at the eyes of its attacker. The venom incapacitates the predator, temporarily blinding it. The zebra spitting cobra also has a flattened neck that it can expand when threatened, a trait common to many types of cobra. It has a dark brown body with light stripes, a pattern that resembles a zebra.

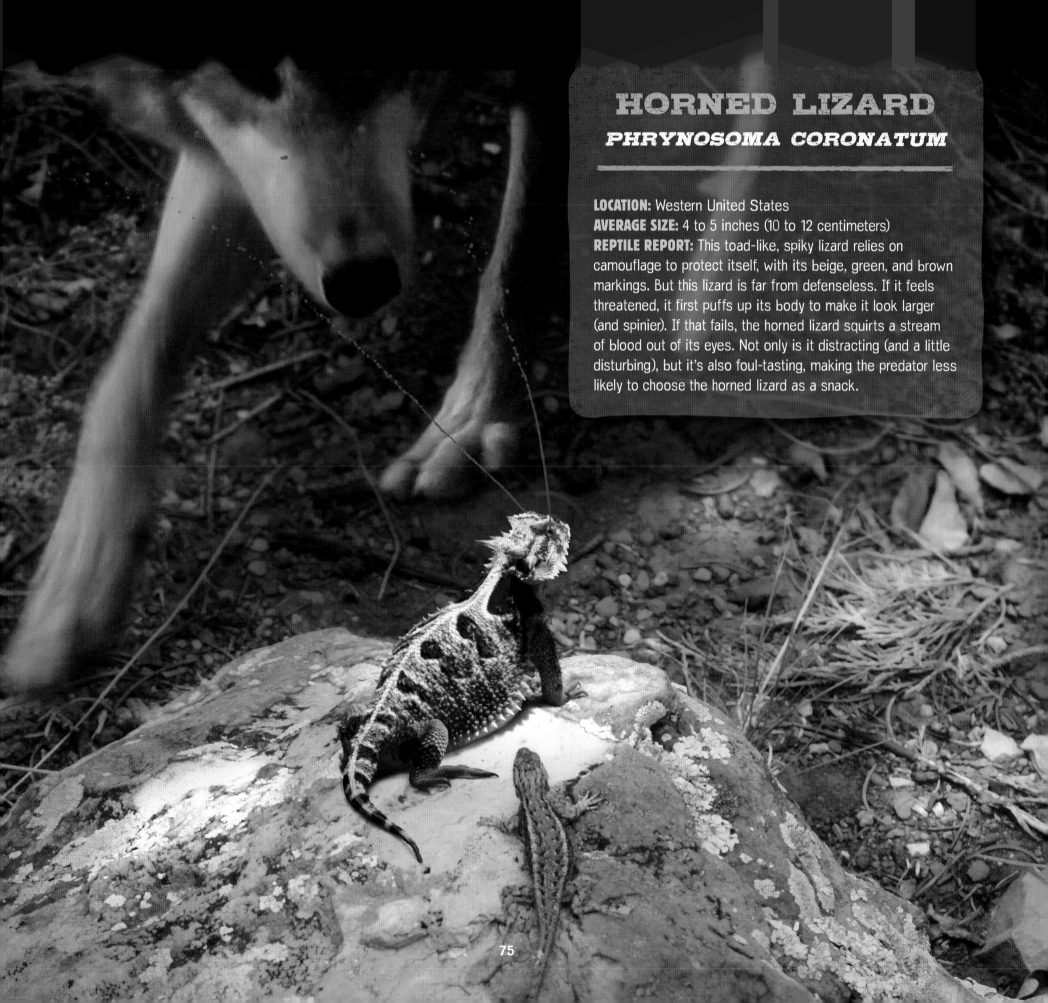

HORNED LIZARD
PHRYNOSOMA CORONATUM

LOCATION: Western United States
AVERAGE SIZE: 4 to 5 inches (10 to 12 centimeters)
REPTILE REPORT: This toad-like, spiky lizard relies on camouflage to protect itself, with its beige, green, and brown markings. But this lizard is far from defenseless. If it feels threatened, it first puffs up its body to make it look larger (and spinier). If that fails, the horned lizard squirts a stream of blood out of its eyes. Not only is it distracting (and a little disturbing), but it's also foul-tasting, making the predator less likely to choose the horned lizard as a snack.

EASTERN CORAL SNAKE
MICRURUS FULVUS

LOCATION: Southeastern United States
AVERAGE SIZE: 3 to 4 feet (1 meter)
REPTILE REPORT: Coral reefs are famous for their vibrant colors, and the coral snake is named after reefs because of its brightly colored stripes of yellow, red, and black. But even though the colors of a reef are a sign of beauty, the colors of a coral snake are a warning that these snakes are venomous. There are a few different species of coral snakes that share the same markings, a natural phenomenon called Müllerian mimicry.

The eastern coral snake is native to the coastal states of the Southeastern United States, but they're not often seen because they spend most of their time underground. They hunt other snakes and lizards, injecting them with venom to incapacitate their prey. Because of their markings, it's hard to tell which end is the tail and which end is the head. The coral snake uses that to its advantage when threatened, swinging its tail in a way that mimics a head. It's unlikely for a human to be bitten by a coral snake since they're so secretive, but if it does happen the venom can be very dangerous if left untreated.

SONORAN MOUNTAIN KINGSNAKE
LAMPROPELTIS PYROMELANA

LOCATION: Western United States
AVERAGE SIZE: 3 feet (1 meter)
REPTILE REPORT: The Sonoran mountain kingsnake has black and red markings on its body to make it look like a coral snake. The mountain snake prefers the elevation and rocky terrain of mountainous areas, and it's an excellent climber that's sometimes spotted in trees or up on boulders. Unlike the coral snake, which uses venom to hunt, the Sonoroan mountain kingsnake is a constrictor, which means it kills lizards, rodents, and birds by coiling its body tightly around its prey.

FALSE CORAL SNAKE
ERYTHROLAMPRUS AESCULAPII

LOCATION: South America
AVERAGE SIZE: 5 feet (1½ meters)
REPTILE REPORT: Similar to Müllerian mimicry, there's another type of mimicry called Batesian mimicry. But instead of similar species sharing traits as a warning, Batesian mimics are a little more deceptive because they do not share the dangerous trait of the species they mimic. For example, false coral snakes are mildly venomous, but they're far less dangerous than true coral snakes even though they have similar markings and colorings. That's because false coral snakes adapted to look like the dangerous coral snake. Predators know to avoid those colors if they want to avoid the more dangerous coral snake, so the false coral snake is safer.

77

CALABAR BURROWING BOA
CALABARIA REINHARDTII

LOCATION: Africa

AVERAGE SIZE: 3 feet (1 meter)

REPTILE REPORT: Boas are a family of snakes known for killing their prey by constriction, which means they coil their body tightly around the prey. For the Calabar burrowing boas, causing confusion is the best defense. When a predator approaches, the Calabar burrowing boa curls up into a tight ball, hiding its head under the coils of its body. Then, it lifts its tail in the air and waves it around. The patterns on its tail look like a head, confusing predators into thinking this snake is ready to attack when it's really hiding.

The Calabar burrowing boa lives buried under leaves, logs, and other forest debris. They like to eat small rodents, and will burrow into the ground to find them. They have an incredibly thick, almost armor-like skin. Scientists debate whether the Calabar burrowing boa belongs to the same family as python snakes or as boa snakes, since it seems to share some characteristics of both families of snakes, but most recently they think it best fits in with the boas.

SRI LANKAN PIPESNAKE
CYLINDROPHIS MACULATUS

LOCATION: Sri Lanka

AVERAGE SIZE: 12 to 14 inches (30 to 35 centimeters)

REPTILE REPORT: In the movie *Aladdin*, when Jafar turns into a giant snake, the sides of his neck stick out and look like a hood. That's how you can tell Jafar is a cobra. Cobras have a flattened neck that alerts predators that they're dangerous. But the Sri Lankan pipesnake isn't a cobra, and it isn't very dangerous. It can't flatten its neck the way a cobra can; instead, the Sri Lankan pipesnake flattens out its tail and lifts it up to make a fake cobra head. It keeps its real head tucked under its body to sell the ruse. The Sri Lankan pipesnake is hoping the attacker will be tricked enough to leave it alone. Its black and red coloring is another defense to prevent predators from getting too close.

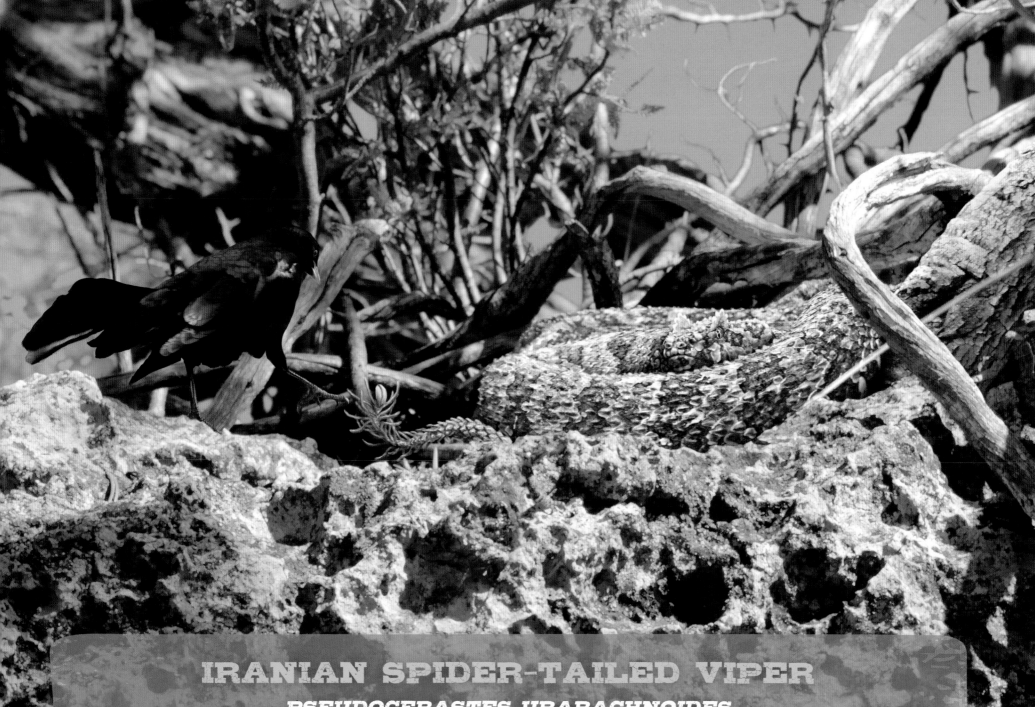

IRANIAN SPIDER-TAILED VIPER
PSEUDOCERASTES URARACHNOIDES

LOCATION: Iran and Iraq

AVERAGE SIZE: 2 to 3 feet (¾ meter)

REPTILE REPORT: If you're not a fan of spiders, you'll want to stay away from this snake. The Iranian spider-tailed viper has a unique hunting method that mimics another of the world's greatest ew-inducing creatures: a spider. This viper's tail looks like a spider, legs and all, and it will use its camouflage colors to blend in with the ground and then move that tail around. This trick is meant to lure in birds and other critters that eat spiders by tricking them into thinking there's no snake there, just a tasty spider snack. Once its prey is close enough, the Iranian spider-tailed viper pounces.

CROSSED PIT VIPER
BOTHROPS ALTERNATUS

LOCATION: South America

AVERAGE SIZE: 3 to 4 feet (1 meter)

REPTILE REPORT: This snake would love a "Do Not Disturb" sign. The crossed pit viper is a nocturnal, tropical snake that favors open fields or marshes, but it does not like to be approached. If it's disturbed, its first line of defense is to hide its head, making it seem like it's not going to react. But it will quickly attack if the threat doesn't leave. With its brown and black patterned body, this snake looks like a nonvenomous boa constrictor (which relies on constricting to hunt instead of the venom vipers use). But the coloring is just a ploy to prevent other animals from bothering it. The crossed pit viper is actually a very venomous, dangerous viper, not a boa. Like other pit vipers, it has pit organs that allow them to sense the body heat of the small mammals they like to eat.

SOUTHERN CORAL SNAKE
MICRURUS FRONTALIS

LOCATION: South America
AVERAGE SIZE: 3 to 5 feet (1 to 1½ meters)
REPTILE REPORT: Not all venomous snakes want to attack, and the southern coral snake is a great example. Despite having a painful, venomous bite, the southern coral snake prefers not to be approached at all. Its colors serve as a warning to keep away, but if a predator does approach, this snake will curl up into a ball to protect its head and wave its tail around to distract and intimidate the threat. Attacking is its last resort, and it's an incredibly successful one since the southern coral snake has an often deadly bite.

SOUTH AMERICAN HOGNOSE SNAKE
LYSTROPHIS DORBIGNYI

LOCATION: South America
AVERAGE SIZE: 1 to 2 feet (½ meter)
REPTILE REPORT: Have you ever seen someone do a really good impression? With its brown, gray, and tan markings, the South American hognose snake does its best impression of a crossed pit viper to try to keep itself safe. But that's not the only bigger, badder snake it imitates. When threatened, the South American hognose snake will also move its body, flatten itself, and coil up and display its tail in motions similar to the southern coral snake. Some hognose snakes have also developed reddish markings that look a little like the coral snake's distinctive coloring.

CHAPTER 5

SUPERLATIVES

There are so many reptiles in nature, and they all have interesting skills and personalities, so it's hard to compare them or rank them. But there are some reptiles that stand out from the rest, with extraordinary skills, sizes, and looks.

Most yearbooks have a section of superlatives in them, where class members pick the "best" fit for fun categories. Someone could have the Most School Spirit or be the Class Clown. In this chapter, you'll find the best of the best in the reptile world. There are creatures that are the biggest, the prickliest, the oldest, and more.

LEAF CHAMELEON
BROOKESIA MICRA

LOCATION: Madagascar
AVERAGE SIZE: ½ to 1 inch (2 centimeters)
REPTILE REPORT: Did you know that an American quarter is just under 1-inch wide? That means that even the largest leaf chameleon would only be about as long as the width of a quarter. Chameleons are well-known for being excellent at hiding, but this tiny lizard's size takes its camouflage one step further. At night, these minuscule lizards sleep motionless and hidden on branches that are just a few inches off the ground. They live in just one small section of Madagascar, and during the day they walk around on the forest floor.

Their small size undoubtedly puts them in danger, but an even bigger threat is the deforestation of their home. Since they only live in a small area, losing part of their habitat could be devastating. Their habitat might also be a reason for their small size. Insular dwarfism is a scientific phenomenon where species that live in contained areas like islands evolve to be smaller than similar species that live on the mainland because the resources on an island are much more limited.

SALTWATER CROCODILE
CROCODYLUS POROSUS

BIGGEST

LOCATION: Australia, New Guinea, and Indonesia

AVERAGE SIZE: Males, 17 to 20 feet (5 to 6 meters); females, 8 to 9 feet (2½ meters)

REPTILE REPORT: Steve Irwin, Australia's famed Crocodile Hunter, absolutely loved crocodiles. In fact, he loved them so much that he named his daughter, Bindi Irwin, after his favorite animal at the Australia Zoo—a female saltwater crocodile he rescued named Bindi. Crocodiles have a bit of a bad reputation because of their massive size. Male saltwater crocodiles are the largest reptiles alive, and their scaly appearance, visible teeth, and large, clawed feet add to their intimidating appearance. Although the saltwater crocodile typically prefers coastal water, they can also be found in freshwater rivers and swamps to raise their young (females can lay an average of 40 to 60 eggs). They use the water to regulate their temperature, sinking below the surface with just their eyes and nostrils exposed when they need to cool down and basking on rocks in the sun to warm up.

The saltwater crocodile isn't just one of the biggest reptiles, it's also one of the most intelligent. Saltwater crocodiles use different sounds to communicate with one another, letting out a bark or a growl to warn other crocodiles of danger or to find mates. Because of its large size, the saltwater crocodile is an impressive hunter. They submerge themselves under the water to stalk their prey (which can be anything from snakes and birds to monkeys and buffalo) and then lunge to drag it under the water.

TUATARA
SPHENODON PUNCTATUS

LONGEST LINEAGE

LOCATION: New Zealand and surrounding islands

AVERAGE SIZE: Male, 24 inches (60 centimeters); female, 15 inches (38 centimeters)

REPTILE REPORT: Imagine being the last remaining member of your family. It's a lonely thought, but for the tuatara it's a reality. The tuatara is the last remaining species of an ancient family of reptiles called *Rhynchocephalia*. Fossils of other members of the *Rhynchocephalia* order date back as far as 240 million years ago in the Triassic Period. Now, only the tuatara remains, living on the cool, windy cliffs on the islands around New Zealand. It's not just their family that's incredibly old; an individual tuatara can live for more than 100 years. They make their homes in burrows and are nocturnal, but they can sometimes be seen basking in the sun near the entrance of their burrow to warm up. They have an incredibly slow metabolism, so they don't need to eat frequently, but when they do they hunt for small insects, birds, rodents, frogs, or other lizards.

The concept of a "third eye" is sometimes considered to be spiritual, mystical, or supernatural, but for the tuatara the third eye is literal. They have two eyes and a small opening on their head called a parietal eye. The parietal eye doesn't function like a normal eye since the tuatara grows scales to cover it, but it's a sensory organ that helps them maintain their temperature.

GIANT TORTOISE
CHELONOIDIS DUNCANENSIS

LOCATION: Galápagos Islands

AVERAGE SIZE: 4 to 5 feet (1 to 1½ meters)

REPTILE REPORT: Let's take a trip back to the start of the 1830s. No cell phones, no television, no video games. Andrew Jackson was the seventh president of the U.S.—and the U.S. only had 24 recognized states. That's the decade when scientists estimate Harriet, a giant tortoise from the Galápagos Islands, was born. Harriet was transported to the Australia Zoo where she lived until she passed away in 2006. Scientists aren't sure of Harriet's exact birthday, but they guess she was anywhere from 170 to 175 years old when she died.

    The giant tortoise is one of the longest-living creatures on Earth. They live a fairly lazy life, eating leaves and basking in the sun, and napping for as much as 16 hours a day. In the wild, they can live for more than 100 years, and because of their large size and thick protective shell, there aren't many predators that threaten them once they're fully grown. But other animals on the island can threaten their food supply, and plenty of animals seek out giant tortoise eggs as a snack, making it hard for the giant tortoise to reproduce. All species of giant tortoise, including the one native to the Galápagos Islands, are on the endangered species list. There have been lots of efforts to breed the turtles in captivity and release them when they're large enough to protect themselves, but human activity in their natural habitat is still a threat to their survival.

OLDEST LIVING

THORNY DEVIL
MOLOCH HORRIDUS

PRICKLIEST

LOCATION: Australia

AVERAGE SIZE: 6 to 8 inches (15 to 20 centimeters)

REPTILE REPORT: The name devil might have you thinking of pointy horns and pitchforks. And although the thorny devil doesn't have a pitchfork, it does have plenty of horns—or, really, spines. These spines cover its body like armor, which is especially protective since this little lizard is only a few inches long. The largest spine on the back of its neck works as a false head. If a predator attacks, the thorny lizard will duck its real head down to protect itself and distracts the predator with the fake head. In addition to its spines, the thorny devil is also defended by impressive camouflage. They live in sandy soil and deserts, and their brown, spotted coloring helps them blend into the sand.

Their spines aren't just for protection. Water clings to their textured bodies better, helping them maintain their body temperature, and the spines are thought to help them direct the water right into their mouths to make drinking easier. Thorny devils have a slow, deliberate walk, and they only eat ants.

ARABIAN SAND BOA
ERYX JAYAKARI

LOCATION: Middle East, North Africa, and West Asia

AVERAGE SIZE: 15 to 16 inches (38 to 40 centimeters)

REPTILE REPORT: Have you ever made a sock puppet? You slip a sock over your hand, maybe adding some googly eyes, and then you use your fingers as a mouth. This snake's head has been called a "sock-puppet" face because it's almost cartoonish. It has big, round, raised eyes on the top of its head rather than on the side like most other snakes. And although it might look cute, those eyes are really to help it hunt. The sand boa lives in desert environments and burrows down into the sand during the day. It hunts at night, keeping its body under the sand and leaving just its eyes above the surface to watch for prey. Its beige coloring helps camouflage it even further, making it unnoticeable in the sand. When lizards or small rodents approach, the sand boa ambushes its prey.

GOOFIEST

ELEPHANT TRUNK SNAKE
ACROCHORDUS JAVANICUS

LOCATION: Southeast Asia

AVERAGE SIZE: Males, 5 feet (1½ meters); females, 8 feet (2½ meters)

REPTILE REPORT: Picture an elephant's trunk. It's large and thick, and it has lots of folds in the skin that make it look saggy and loose. That's what the elephant trunk snake looks like. It has a thick, brown body with skin that's loose and baggy.

This aquatic snake prefers rivers and streams, but it will sometimes swim into the sea. Its skin is a benefit for swimming, helping it move through the water quickly. But because their skin is so well adapted to the water, these snakes don't do well on land, and they rarely come out of the water fully. Instead, they spend most of their time in the muddy water, just floating up toward the surface and lifting their nose out for a breath when necessary. It's nonvenomous, so instead it waits patiently to ambush its prey, which is usually fish, small aquatic animals, or frogs.

FLABBIEST

STRETCHIEST

INDIAN NARROW HEADED SOFTSHELL TURTLE
CHITRA INDICA

LOCATION: South Asia

AVERAGE SIZE: 2 to 3 feet (¾ meter)

REPTILE REPORT: Some turtles have the ability to pull their whole body into their shell—this turtle can do the opposite, extending its neck out long in front of it, and making it look more like a giraffe than a turtle. The neck extension is a hunting tactic, and this freshwater ambush predator will wait in the sandy rivers where it lives and quickly shoot its neck out to catch fish or other aquatic animals swimming by. Its bite is quick and powerful, and the force of its head jutting out has even been known to damage small fishing boats that it bumps while hunting. Unlike typical turtles with a hard shell, this softshell turtle has leather-like skin.

CHAPTER 6

ENDANGERED REPTILES

Nature is constantly changing, evolving, and adapting. There are a lot of reasons why a species might go extinct. Animals adapt to live in a certain temperature in a certain area with a certain food source, and if any one of those factors changes, it becomes very difficult for that species to survive. Hunting and poaching can have a big impact on a species. When a species is endangered, it is given protections that prevent people from hunting it any more. And although hunting is an active way that humans can endanger animals, there are also indirect ways that people harm the animals on our planet.

Climate change affects just about every animal on the planet, from the smallest organisms to the largest. It destroys habitats, limits food sources, and makes it difficult for species to thrive in a warmer environment. Small amounts of climate change are a natural occurrence, but people make the rising temperatures worse. In fact, scientists have found that humans have been the biggest cause of climate change in the last 100 years. Modern technology like electricity, cars, and factories need a lot of power to run, and they release gases into the air, especially carbon dioxide. Those gases go up into the Earth's atmosphere and trap in heat. Since the heat can't escape from the atmosphere, the Earth's temperature slowly rises. This is called the greenhouse effect (like how a greenhouse keeps in heat for plants), and the more gases there are in the air, the more the temperature rises.

Pollution and deforestation are two other human influences that can hurt animals. Imagine how upset you would be if somebody filled your bedroom with garbage. Or even worse, bulldozed it completely. An animal's home is nature, and when people ruin that home with garbage or destroy it, the animals can't always find a new home that meets their needs.

So what can people do to help these endangered animals? Working to slow down climate change is a big help, along with protecting the homes of these species from human activity. Some environments are even turned into nature preserves or conservation areas where human activity is limited and the natural habitat is protected. These kinds of efforts help every animal in that environment to survive. There are also species-specific programs to help some of the most endangered animals. If a species can't reproduce, it can't survive, so captive breeding programs (like many zoos have) help encourage bigger populations. Plus, young animals struggle to survive in the wild since they're smaller and less protected, so if they're bred in captivity and released back into the wild when they're a little older and bigger, they have a better chance of surviving.

CRITICALLY ENDANGERED

BURMESE STAR TORTOISE

GEOCHELONE PLATYNOTA

LOCATION: Myanmar

AVERAGE SIZE: 12 to 14 inches (30 to 35 centimeters)

REPTILE REPORT: This tortoise gets a gold star for its unique shell design. Yellow geometric lines on its shell make a stunning star-shaped pattern. Tortoises are land-dwellers, and the Burmese star tortoise lives only in Myanmar. It prefers dry areas like pastures and fields and usually eats fruits and flowers, along with some insects.

The Burmese star tortoise is a critically endangered species. Threats to its habitat are a big problem, but the bigger threat is human. This rare tortoise is prized and hunted by humans as a delicacy. Captive breeding programs have helped to get more of these turtles out in the wild, but there are still very few of them left, and they're very much in danger of going extinct.

ENDANGERED
MARY RIVER TURTLE
ELUSOR MACRURUS

LOCATION: Australia

AVERAGE SIZE: 16 to 18 inches (40 to 45 centimeters)

REPTILE REPORT: A turtle with a green mohawk? The Mary River turtle often sports a growth of bright green algae on the top of its head. Mary isn't this turtle's name, but its location. The Mary River turtle is a freshwater turtle that lives only in the Mary River in Australia. Unlike other turtles that have to come up to breathe frequently, this turtle has special glands that allow it to breathe underwater. With this unique skill, the Mary River turtle can stay submerged under the water for up to 3 days without needing to come up for air.

This endangered turtle was once prized as a pet, and the illegal collection of the eggs to sell as pets—along with new dams and changes to their river habitat—has endangered this species. Because it was so common as a pet, it's sometimes called the "penny turtle" or the "pet shop turtle." Now, it's considered protected, and there are conservation and breeding programs to help protect it from going extinct.

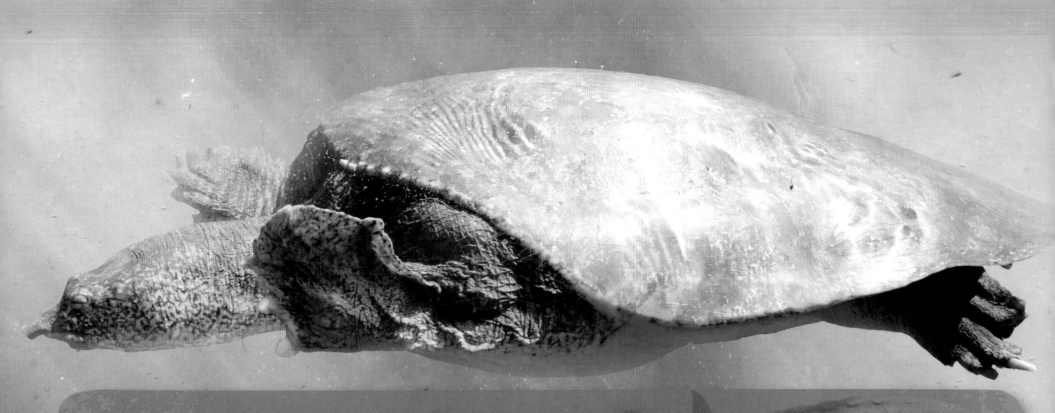

YANGTZE GIANT SOFTSHELL TURTLE
RAFETUS SWINHOEI

LOCATION: Vietnam and China
AVERAGE SIZE: 3 feet (1 meter)
REPTILE REPORT: The rarest of reptiles, this turtle is so endangered that its population is in the single digits. As far as scientists know, as of this writing in 2020, there are only three in existence. There are two living in the wild in Vietnam, and one lives in captivity in China. The wild turtles in Vietnam live in lakes, and scientists are desperately hoping that more will be found hidden in other lakes. If not, this turtle is unfortunately doomed to extinction. The turtle in captivity is male, and scientists don't know the gender of the two turtles in Vietnam. Unless there's a female somewhere in the wild, there's no chance of these turtles being able to reproduce. So how did things get this dire for the Yangtze giant softshell? There was a period of time when human activity caused a lot of changes in the Yangtze River (the location that gives this turtle its name). Areas were dammed off, changing the shape of the river and cutting off animals from other members of their species. The Yangtze giant softshell turtle isn't the only species that has suffered in this region. The Baji river dolphin (*Lipotes vexillifer*) and the Chinese paddlefish (*Psephurus gladius*) are both incredibly endangered species living in the Yangtze River system.

Because scientists haven't been able to study many up close, we don't know much about them, but based on the animals ... been able to study from a distance they think that the ... ...tshell turtle might be the world's largest freshwater turtle— ...ligator snapping turtle (see page 33).

CRITICALLY ENDANGERED

HAWKSBILL SEA TURTLE

ERETMOCHELYS IMBRICATA

LOCATION: Atlantic Ocean, Indian Ocean, and Pacific Ocean

AVERAGE SIZE: 2 to 3 feet (¾ meter)

REPTILE REPORT: In the brightly colored reefs of shallow tropical waters, the hawksbill sea turtle swims looking for sea sponges, fish, mollusks, algae, and other plants. Their name comes from their pointed, bird-like beak. Hawksbill turtles are relatively small compared to other sea turtles.

Habitat loss and human hunting are the two biggest threats to this species. Those beautiful coral reefs that the hawksbill relies on for food are disappearing thanks to climate change. And people have historically hunted this turtle for its prized shell and meat. They're listed as a critically endangered species, and conservationists are looking for ways to protect the hawksbill and its marine habitat.

CRITICALLY ENDANGERED
WHITE CAY ROCK IGUANA
CYCLURA RILEYI CRISTATA

LOCATION: Bahamas
AVERAGE SIZE: 10 to 12 inches (25 to 30 centimeters)
REPTILE REPORT: Sun, surf, and sand—this iguana is living the island life in the Bahamas. But sleeping on the beach isn't all it's cracked up to be. In fact, it's a big part of why this iguana is endangered. The White Cay rock iguana lives only on one island in the Bahamas, White Cay. They used to be more widely distributed on other islands in the region, but now there aren't many left. As the islands became more inhabited, rats and feral raccoons started appearing, killing the iguanas. In the late 1990s, scientists estimated there were fewer than 200 White Cay rock iguanas left. Conservationists have done a lot of work to reduce the rat problem, but these iguanas don't reproduce very often. Females only lay two to three eggs per year, so scientists aren't sure when (or if) the population will grow in size.

This brownish-orange iguana is relatively small compared to other iguanas. It's an herbivore, eating leaves, flowers, and fruits native to the island.

WAGNER'S VIPER
MONTIVIPERA WAGNERI

LOCATION: Turkey and Iran
AVERAGE SIZE: 1½ to 2 feet (½ meter)
REPTILE REPORT: If you've ever gone hiking, you know that the view from atop a mountain or a hill is a beautiful sight. Wagner's viper would definitely agree—its home is nearly 10,000 feet above sea level. Their elevated environment is usually rocky, and although it's warm during the day the temperatures drop at night.

Scientists thought this snake was extinct for nearly 140 years. But in 1983, some were discovered in the wild. It has lost a lot of its habitat, and it's hunted by rare animal collectors. There are breeding programs in zoos to help keep Wagner's viper from going extinct, but the threats to their environment mean that they might not have a home much longer.

SHORT-NOSED SEA SNAKE
AIPYSURUS APRAEFRONTALIS

LOCATION: Australia

AVERAGE SIZE: 1–2 feet (½ meter)

REPTILE REPORT: Can you imagine staying underwater for almost two hours? Humans would need scuba diving equipment to explore the Ashmore and Hibernia reefs off the western coast of Australia, but the short-nosed sea snake has adapted to living in this coral. They still need to come up to the surface to breathe, but they can stay underwater anywhere from 30 minutes to two hours. The short-nosed sea snake is venomous and hunts fish and eels hiding in the reef. This dark brown snake with a small, pointed head lives only in these two reefs, but they're separated by deep water that's too hard for the snakes to cross. This separation makes it hard for the snakes to find mates, but that's not the biggest threat to their survival. The reefs where this snake lives are disappearing. Climate change has made the water warmer, which damages the coral and harms the snakes that have adapted to live in cooler water.

MONA ISLAND BOA
CHILABOTHRUS MONENSIS

LOCATION: Puerto Rico

AVERAGE SIZE: 3 feet (1 meter)

REPTILE REPORT: Stories of shipwrecks on deserted islands make them seem like intimidating places, but islands without people are home to some of the world's most spectacular animals and natural landscapes. That's certainly the case with Puerto Rico's Mona Island—other than a few rangers and scientists, no people live there. That's because Mona Island is a nature preserve where visitors can learn about the unique species that live there. The Mona Island boa has always been rare. It only lives on this island, where it feeds on lizards and mice. Like other snakes it's nocturnal, but unlike other snakes the Mona Island boa gives birth to live young instead of laying eggs.

Because the Mona Island boa only lives on one island, it's very threatened by changes to its habitat. Before the island became a nature preserve, wild pigs, goats, and cats were introduced to the environment, and they became predators of the Mona Island boa. But now that the island habitat is more protected, scientists are working to control the population of these predators to save the island's native species. Zoos around the world also have breeding programs to help prevent the Mona Island boa from going extinct.

GHARIAL

GAVIALIS GANGETICUS

LOCATION: India

AVERAGE SIZE: 16 to 20 feet (5 to 6 meters)

REPTILE REPORT: Have you ever gotten a piggyback ride? A gharial will sometimes give its kids a lift while they swim. Although there are many species of reptiles that don't spend much time with their young, gharials will spend a few weeks with their kids. And they have a lot of kids—females can lay around 60 eggs at once. Gharials live in fast-flowing, freshwater rivers in India. They don't move very well on land, but they come up to the shore or sandbars to bask in the sun. The name gharial comes from the word "ghara," which is what the rounded part at the end of their long, narrow snout is called.

With so many offspring, it's hard to imagine how the gharial could go extinct. But scientists think there may be fewer than 200 left. The biggest threat is changes to the rivers where they live. Dams in the rivers separate the gharials, making it impossible for them to find other gharials for mating. And fishing activity in the rivers can accidentally harm the eggs and young gharials. Hunting is also a big threat to the gharial population. Though they're now protected, gharials and their eggs were once heavily hunted by locals.

CRITICALLY ENDANGERED

ORINOCO CROCODILE
CROCODYLUS INTERMEDIUS

LOCATION: Colombia and Venezuela

AVERAGE SIZE: 10 to 15 feet (3 to 4½ meters)

REPTILE REPORT: The Orinoco River winds its way through the rainforests of South America, providing a habitat for countless animals. It's the home to one of the rarest reptiles in the world, the Orinoco crocodile. Like other freshwater crocodiles, the Orinoco crocodile spends most of its time in the water, using the nostrils at the end of its long snout to help it breathe. In the dry season when the river is low, it will live in burrows near the riverbanks.

Changes to the river and the rainforests around it are a big threat to the Orinoco crocodile's survival. They used to have a much larger area to live in, but the loss of the rainforests and manmade changes to the river have limited them. Although they're now protected, in the early 1900s this crocodile was hunted by humans for its valuable skin. The population decreased so much that it hasn't been able to rebound.

104

AMERICAN ALLIGATOR

ALLIGATOR MISSISSIPPIENSIS

LOCATION: Southeast United States

AVERAGE SIZE: 9 to 12 feet (2¾ to 3½ meters)

REPTILE REPORT: Stories of alligators in swimming pools or neighborhood ponds might sound scary, but it's actually a good sign that this species is surviving. The American alligator was nearly extinct about 50 years ago, but captive breeding programs helped to stabilize the population. This freshwater alligator lives in rivers, marshes, swamps, and ponds in the southeast United States. It spends most of its time in the water, but it can make a burrow in the ground, called a gator hole, if there's a drought and it needs to protect itself until more water is available. Alligators are a social species that usually lives in small groups, which helps to protect them from predators. Alligators will eat just about anything from fish to reptiles to birds. Scientists have noticed that they'll sometimes even eat rocks or bottle caps! The biggest difference between an alligator and a crocodile is its teeth. Crocodiles have a smile—the teeth on their lower jaw are always visible—but when an alligator closes its mouth those big bottom teeth aren't visible. Even though you can't always see them, alligators have plenty of teeth (up to 80 in their mouth at once). Those teeth wear down and fall out kind of like losing baby teeth, but the process happens a lot more frequently throughout their life; they can go through about 3,000 teeth over the course of their life!

Living around humans provides lots of threats both on land and in the water. Cars, boats, and fishing nets can injure or kill alligators accidentally. Hunting and habitat loss also contributed to the alligator's near extinction. It's no easy task to bring a species back from the brink of extinction. The alligator's success came from a combination of protections, including breeding programs and habitat protection.

CHAPTER 7

LIVING JEWELS

f you blow a bubble from soap and look at it, it's really hard to describe its color, because it reflects back a shiny rainbow on its surface. The bubble is iridescent, a phenomenon where the light and the angle make it look like the bubble changes colors. There are lots of naturally occurring iridescent things in nature, including reptiles.

To understand what causes iridescence in animals, we need to talk about how people see colors. Color is really all about light. An animal's skin (or scales) will absorb some light wavelengths and reflect back some. The wavelengths that are reflected back determine what color you see when you look at the animal. But instead of just absorbing and reflecting the light, iridescence happens when the structure of the animal's skin (or scales) interferes with the light wavelengths, making them overlap each other in an unusual way and causing you to see different colors from different angles.

That's exactly what would happen if you were to look at a sunbeam snake (*Xenopeltis unicolor*). Under shadowed lighting its scales can look brown, but when bright light hits it (like sunlight or a camera flash) the snake's body turns iridescent. The same is true with the white-lipped python (*Bothrochilus albertisii*), and its rainbow colors are even more visible on its normally black scales. The iridescence can even happen on snakes with patterned scales. The rainbow boa (*Epicrates assisi*) has a series of brown circular patterns on its body, but in the light its rainbow sheen shows.

Those cool colors are spectacular to look at, but it makes you wonder why these snakes would want to be iridescent in the first place. Scientists have a few theories. The structures in the scales that make it iridescent can also make the scales water-repellent. So it's kind of like these snakes are always wearing a raincoat. The scales might also be stronger. Because they're slick, the scales help snakes burrow better; less dirt sticks to the snake, and there's less friction between the snake and the ground so they can burrow more efficiently. They could be a way to send messages to other members of the same species, using the light and colors to communicate with a potential mate or warn others about predators. The sheen of iridescent animals could also serve as a sort of camouflage in muddy or wet areas, since water is reflective.

White-lipped python
Bothrochilus albertisii

Rainbow boa
Epicrates assisi

Sunbeam snake
Xenopeltis unicolor

109

Gold dust day gecko
Phelsuma laticauda

Black-spotted least gecko
Sphaerodactylus nigropunctatus

The phrase "all the colors of the rainbow" couldn't be more true for these lizards. They exist in every color from red to green to blue, including every shade in between. Color can mean a lot of different things in animals, but with lizards it's usually one of the two C's: camouflage and communication. Many lizards share the colors of nature, like the greens, browns, yellows, and even reds you would expect to see in a forest or a desert. But not all lizards have camouflage colors, and some are as bright as the colors of the rainbow. When it comes to brighter colors, it's more often about socializing or communicating with other lizards. The colors could be a signal to help the lizards identify mates. Some lizards will even change color throughout their life. Many young lizards are a different color when they're young than they are as adults, and some lizards (like chameleons and anoles) have the ability to change their colors based on the social situation—the color change can let other members of the species know they're ready to mate, or it can warn other animals that this lizard is marking its territory and feels threatened.

Some species are all red or orange, like Geyr's spiny-tailed lizard (*Uromastyx geyri*) from North Africa, and some are solid green, like the gold dust day gecko (*Phelsuma laticauda*)—this lizard is kind of a celebrity, since it inspired the gecko that's the mascot for Geico insurance. But not all lizards are just one color. Some have bold patterns like the blue and

South Indian Rock Agama
Psammophilus dorsalis

Panther chameleon
Furcifer pardalis

Geyr's spiny-tailed lizard
Uromastyx geyri

green markings of the peacock day gecko (*Phelsuma quadriocellata parva*). And there are lots of lizards with stripes. Patterns don't have to be uniform on the lizards' bodies. Sometimes just the head is colored. These colors can be striking, like the half pink, half blue Mwanza flat-headed rock agama (*Agama mwanzae*).

And not all lizards of the same species are the same color, because coloring is sometimes used to show which gender is which. This can help the lizards find a mate by communicating gender to other lizards of the same species, like how the male Williams' dwarf gecko (*Lygodactylus williamsi*) is blue. Male Peninsular rock agama (*Psammophilus dorsalis*) have a red or orange band for mating. Color differences can also sometimes show you where that lizard is from, like how the male panther chameleon (*Furcifer pardalis*) has different colors and patterns based on where in Madagascar they're from. And it's not just the males that have bright color differences. For the Lesser chameleon (*Furcifer minor*), females are more colorful with green and yellow stripes and some violet and red, and with the three-banded gecko (*Sphaerodactylus nigropunctatus*) it's the females that have black stripes with beige and yellow.

Williams' Dwarf Gecko
Lygodactylus williamsi

Peacock Day Gecko
Phelsuma quadriocellata

Mwanza flat-headed agama
Agama mwanzae

Lesser chameleon
Furcifer minor

111

Sinai agama
Pseudotrapelus sinaitus

Yellow sea snake
Hydrophis platurus xanthos

Mud snake
Farancia abacura

Centralian carpet python
Morelia bredli

Black-banded trinket snake
Oreocryptophis porphyraceus

Banded krait
Bungarus fasciatus

Emerald tree boa
Corallus caninus

When a construction worker or a police officer wants to keep people away from a dangerous area, they put up caution tape. The yellow and black colors serve as a warning: stay alert, there's danger. Some snakes have "caution tape" colors, like the black and yellow stripes of the banded krait (*Bungarus fasciatus*). This snake wants you to stay away, but if that warning fails it uses venom for protection. The brilliant solid yellow sea snake (*Hydrophis platurus xanthos*) has similar bold markers.

When it comes to snakes, there are a lot of different colors and patterns, and they can be as subtle as a brown, muddy color, or as bold as the stripes of a coral snake (see page 76). Some are even patterned with black and white markings that look more like a Dalmatian than a snake, like the black false boa (*Pseudoboa nigra*). Like lizards and other reptiles, the more natural colors, like browns or greens, are often a reflection of their natural habitat. The colors of the Asian green ratsnake (*Ptyas nigromarginata*) aren't too surprising. These green snakes mostly live in the forest, where green trees and shrubs can provide them with a place to hide.

With snakes, it's the bright colors that are the most interesting. When a snake stands out from its surroundings it's usually a warning—their colors are a bold, neon sign telling potential predators "stay away, I'm dangerous." And like the venomous banded krait, sometimes that warning is very true. With a black body, blue stripe, and red head and tail, the coloring of the Malaysian blue coral snake (*Maticora bivirgata*) is very interesting to look at. And that's because those colors serve as a warning that it's very venomous: it can even kill humans. Those patterns help it keep attackers away. If it's threatened, it lifts its tail up, which looks just like it's head, to tell the predator to back away. But there are also lots of less-dangerous snakes that adopt bright colors as a way to mimic more dangerous snakes. By faking out potential predators, they're safer. The mud snake (*Farancia abacura*) looks very intimidating with its red and black stripes, but it's actually nonvenomous. Even though they're not as dangerous as venomous snakes, these patterned snakes are more protected because predators are less likely to approach. There are plenty of other red-bodied snakes, like the red bamboo snake (*Oreocryptophis porphyraceus*) with similar warning markings.

Color can be a sign of age, and there are some snakes that are a different color when they're young than they are as an adult. The adult emerald green tree boa (*Corallus caninus*) has a bright green body with white markings, but the young members of this tree snake species are rarely green. They're usually red or orange until they're about a year old, when they turn green. Location is another reason for color differences. The color variance can even be drastic, like in the lesser Sundas pitviper (*Trimeresurus insularis*). This tree-dwelling, venomous snake is typically green or yellowish in color, but there's a group on Komodo Island that's blue.

Asian green rat snake
Ptyas nigromarginata

Malaysian blue coral snake
Maticora bivirgata

Lesser Sunda pit viper
Trimeresurus insularis

Black false boa
Pseudoboa nigra

113

Unlike snakes and lizards, which both typically have scales, turtles are pretty unique in the reptile world. They have a shell that's made up of large, hard scales called scutes. The top of the shell is called the carapace, and the bottom of the shell is called the plastron. Their bodies have dry, scaly skin. Cartoons might make you think a turtle can come all the way out of its shell, but that's not really true. The shell is actually part of their skeleton, so it's always attached. Colors in turtles are usually caused by pigment in their skin or on their shells.

A turtle's color has a lot to do with its habitat. Saltwater turtles that live in warm waters will have much lighter, brighter colors than freshwater turtles living in muddy, sandy waters. And some turtles live on land, so their colors more often reflect the colors around them. Like the mata mata (see page 41), some turtles have colors that match their surroundings as camouflage. The red-crowned roofed turtle (*Batagur kachuga*) has a combination of brown and green colors that help it hide exceptionally well in the dead leaves and debris near the creeks where it lives. The red neck and head are breeding season colors.

The northern red-bellied cooter (*Pseudemys rubriventris*) lives in the United States along the East Coast, and it prefers muddy waters like ponds and rivers. In the winter it will even hibernate in the mud. Young turtles are usually yellow or green, but as they get older they turn darker, reaching a dark brown or black color, and they develop a red striped pattern on its bottom shell. The northern red-bellied cooter isn't the only turtle with red markings. Other semiaquatic turtles have similar coloring, like the northern river terrapin (*Batagur baska*).

Imagine a pair of red eyes staring out at you in the dark. It might sound like a scene out of a horror movie, but there's nothing horrific about eastern box turtles (*Terrapene carolina carolina*). Males have stunning eyes—their irises are bright red! This coloring is a mark of gender, since only the males

Red-crowned roofed turtle
Batagur kachuga

Southern river terrapin
Batagur affinis

Northern river terrapin
Batagur baska

have red eyes. Females typically have yellowish or brown eyes. Their bodies and shells can be a range of colors from brown to orange to reddish in color. Box turtles spend some time on land and some time in the water, and they have high, domed shells.

One of the most endangered turtles, the painted terrapin (*Batagur borneoensis*), is also one of the most uniquely colored. Usually, this turtle isn't much to look at with its brown or black coloring, but when the males are ready to mate they put on a bold display to let the females know. Their shells develop white markings and they get a big red spot in the center of their head, kind of like they put on a red toupee. Breeding and conservation programs are in place to help save this critically endangered turtle from going extinct.

Northern red-bellied turtle
Pseudemys rubriventris

Painted terrapin
Batagur borneoensis

Eastern box turtle
Terrapene carolina

INDEX

INDEX

INDEX

INDEX

About the Illustrator

Julius Csotonyi is one of the world's most high-profile and talented contemporary scientific illustrators. His considerable academic expertise informs his stunning, dynamic art. He has created life-sized dinosaur murals for the Royal Ontario Museum and for the Dinosaur Hall at the Natural History Museum of Los Angeles County, as well as most of the artwork for the exhibit "Deep Time" in the David H. Koch Hall of Fossils at the Smithsonian National Museum of Natural History in Washington, D.C. He lives in Canada.

His books include *Discovering Sharks, Discovering Bugs, The T. Rex Handbook, The Paleoart of Julius Csotonyi,* and *Prehistoric Predators.*

About the Author

Kelly Gauthier is a Boston-based writer and editor.
When she's not working, she can often be found on a boat, in the water, or sitting on the end of a dock reading a book. She is also the author of *Discovering Whales, Discovering Planets and Moons,* and *The Little Chunky Book of Dinosaurs.*

About Applesauce Press

Good ideas ripen with time. From seed to harvest, Applesauce Press creates books with beautiful designs, creative formats, and kid-friendly information. Like our parent company, Cider Mill Press Book Publishers, our press bears fruit twice a year, publishing a new crop of titles each spring and fall.

"Where Good Books Are Ready for Press"
Visit us online at
cidermillpress.com
or write to us at
12 Spring Street, PO Box 454
Kennebunkport, Maine 04046

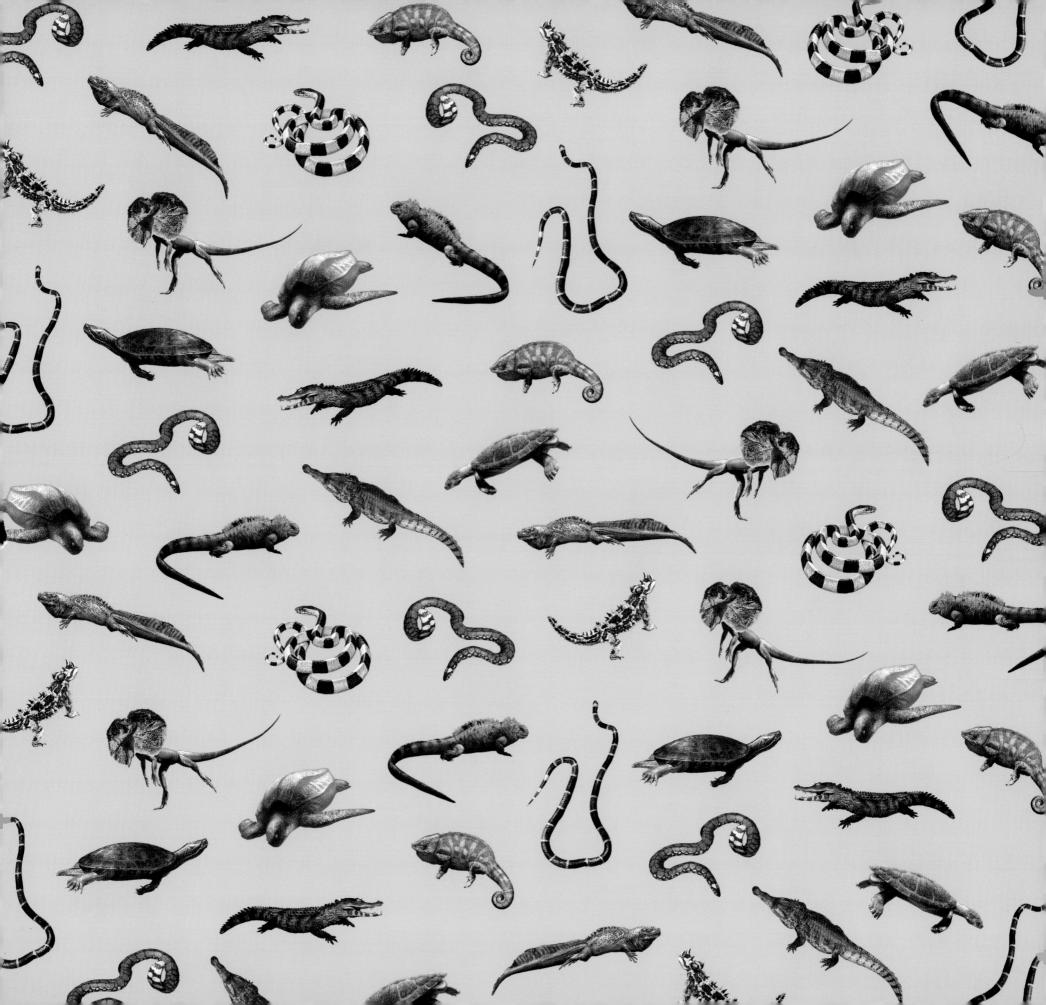

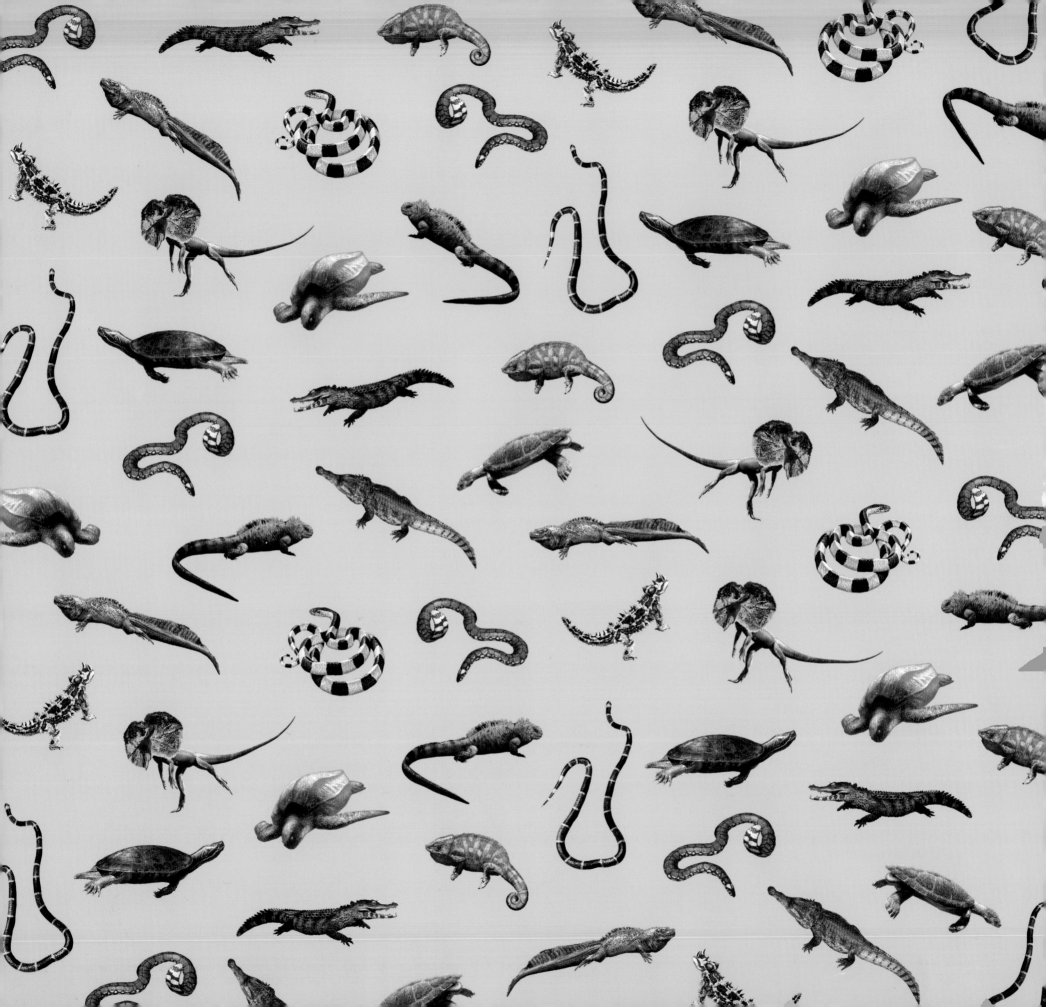